Proofreader's Ma[...]

Mark	Draft	Final

for Refining (continued)

Mark	Draft	Final
;/ Insert semicolon	They expected her to go ⤴;/ however, she did not.	They expected her to go; however, she did not.
:/ Insert colon	. . . ran three tests :/ a, b, and c	. . . ran three tests: a, b, and c.
$\frac{1}{m}$ Insert a dash or change a hyphen to a dash	She won-finally.	She won—finally.
( ) Insert parentheses	Send it today (May 30)	Send it today (May 30).

for Formatting

Mark	Draft	Final
SS [Single-space	SS [He said to come. But I refused.	He said to come. But I refused.
DS [Double-space	DS [He said to come. But I refused.	He said to come. But I refused.
∨ Raise above the line	The 21st day	The 21st day
∧ Drop below the line	H∧2O	H$_2$O
ital. Use italics	The Writing Coach	*The Writing Coach*
bf Use bold face	I will not.	I will **not**.
] Move to the right	] $434.67	$434.67
[Move to the left	[$434.67	$434.67
2] Indent 2 spaces	George Vicas 2] the guest of honor	George Vicas the guest of honor
⟩⟩ Align horizontally	Calling ⟩⟩all campers!	Calling all campers!
‖ Align vertically	‖Ellen Schwartz Richard Rodriguez	Ellen Schwartz Richard Rodriguez
] [Center	]Menu[	Menu
fl Flush left	fl Your honor:	Your honor:
fr Flush right	fr August 7, 200_	August 7, 200_

The Writing Coach

LEE CLARK JOHNS

Strategic Communication, Inc.

THOMSON

DELMAR LEARNING

Australia Canada Mexico Singapore Spain United Kingdom United States

THOMSON
DELMAR LEARNING

The Writing Coach
Lee Clark Johns

Vice President, Career Education SBU:
Dawn Gerrain

Director of Editorial:
Sherry Gomoll

Acquisitions Editor:
Martine Edwards

Developmental Editors:
Patricia Gillivan
Shelley Esposito

Editorial Assistant:
Paul Carmon

Director of Production:
Wendy A. Troeger

Production Coordinator:
Nina Tucciarelli

Cover Design:
Kristina Almquist Design

Channel Manager:
Wendy E. Mapstone

Composition:
Larry O'Brien

For permission to use material from this text or product, contact us by
Tel   (800) 730-2214
Fax   (800) 730-2215
http://www.thomsonrights.com

Library of Congress Cataloging-in-Publication Data

Johns, Lee Clark.
    The writing coach / Lee Clark Johns.
        p. cm.
Includes bibliographical references.
    ISBN 1-4018-3328-4
    I. Authorship. I. Title.
    PN147.J55 2004
    808'.042--dc22

                                    2003017102

NOTICE TO THE READER

Publisher does not warrant or guarantee any of the products described herein or perform any independent analysis in connection with any of the product information contained herein. Publisher does not assume, and expressly disclaims, any obligation to obtain and include information other than that provided to it by the manufacturer.

The reader is expressly warned to consider and adopt all safety precautions that might be indicated by the activities herein and to avoid all potential hazards. By following the instructions contained herein, the reader willingly assumes all risks in connection with such instructions.

The Publisher makes no representation or warranties of any kind, including but not limited to, the warranties of fitness for particular purpose or merchantability, nor are any such representations implied with respect to the material set forth herein, and the publisher takes no responsibility with respect to such material. The Publisher shall not be liable for any special, consequential, or exemplary damages resulting, in whole or part, from the readers' use of, or reliance upon, this material.

DEDICATION

To everyone who "writes for a living"—
which means almost all working adults

Contents

Chapter 5—Editing

Chapter 6—Refining

Chapter 7—Practice

Chapter 8—Fundamentals

Preface

COACHING—THE STRATEGY

A few seasons ago, my favorite basketball team lost its outstanding coach to a bad back for most of the season. It was a disaster. With the same talented, all-American-caliber players, the same seasoned coaching staff, the same rabid fans, the team fell from league leader to basement—and stayed there. Until the coach returned the next season.

Excellent coaches create winners. They identify the talent, develop the plan, and sometimes (but not always) call the plays. These coaches are analytical, strategic, creative, rigorous, and sometimes fun. They produce players who are well-grounded in the basics and make good playing decisions even in the stress of the game.

Like successful coaches, *The Writing Coach* will make you a winner—in your written communication. As a workplace writer or student preparing to enter the workplace, you have the content knowledge and talent. But other members of your team—coworkers, customers, management, vendors, regulators, and the public—need to understand what you know. To ensure that you meet their needs, you will profit from coaching that helps you:

- Move from adequate writing to excellent,
- Ensure that your ideas are clear,
- Prevent misunderstandings and problems,
- Save time in your writing—and rewriting,
- Increase your confidence about your written products.

The goal here is to help you develop strategies, visualize successful options, practice the plays, and learn the rules of effective workplace writing. Then you're ready to win any communication game.

PLAYERS—THE READERS

If you are like the thousands of adults I have taught in business and technical writing seminars for over 25 years, you might introduce yourself like this:

> "I'm a busy adult who is taking this course because I want to improve my writing skills. I have good technical knowledge of (*fill in the blank—engineering, accounting, office services, manufacturing, banking, human resources, information systems, . . .*). I think my writing is okay. At least, no one complains about it.

> "But writing is not my favorite part of the job. It takes more time than I would like, and sometimes I don't know where to begin. I'd like to get rid of the 'fluff.' I'm a little rusty on grammar and know some rules have changed. Plus, people give me conflicting advice. I didn't particularly see the relevance of writing essays in my college classes, so I did just enough to get by.

> "**Now** I know that writing's important. Every promotion brings more responsibility and writing requirements. I don't have time to waste (1) reinventing the wheel with every document, (2) answering follow-up questions, or (3) reworking every document five times. I need some good models, current rules, and an easy-to-use reference."

Unfortunately, books to meet your special requirements as an adult learner are rare. Lengthy business writing textbooks, college handbooks (which can be inconsistent with workplace practice in content and mechanics), short guides addressing one part of the writing process such as editing, formulaic workbooks with fill-in-the-blank drills, and even the venerable *Elements of Style*—none of these fully meet your needs.

PLAYBOOK—*THE WRITING COACH'S* PLAN

The Writing Coach is a practical manual. It walks you through the writing process—from planning, organizing, and writing strategies applied to both long and short documents, to editing and revising the final drafts. Its flexible writing models work in different professions, companies, or organizations. This manual replaces the traditional "how to" texts for different business writing genres (reports, memos, letters) with a commonsense decision-making process that taps your critical thinking skills and experience.

Specifically, *The Writing Coach* offers many useful features.

Easy-to-Follow Structure

■ Five major chapters focused on these steps in the writing process:

Chapter 2, "**Planning**"—Analyzing audience, targeting your purpose, and then brainstorming possible content

Chapter 3, "**Organizing**"—Arranging content logically in all documents—from very long reports and proposals to short letters, memos, and e-mail

Chapter 4, "**Writing**"—Focusing paragraphs to support key points, create logical flow, and add visual clues

Chapter 5, "**Editing**"—Revising for a clear, effective, and concise style

Chapter 6, "**Refining**"—Proofreading for correct sentence structure, grammar, punctuation, and mechanics (This book is formatted based on the style conventions presented here.)

■ Two follow-up chapters:

Chapter 7, "**Practice**"—A Reader-Friendly Writing Checklist; workplace writing scenarios for further practice; additional real-world documents to edit; and self-check answers for the Editing and Refining practice exercises

Chapter 8, "**Fundamentals**"—Including a list of Useful Resources, overviews of key grammar concepts, and a glossary of grammatical terms

■ Tabbed chapter openers containing a Potential Problems-Strategies list and the table of contents for each chapter

■ Chapter overviews summarizing the major points of each chapter

■ Diagrams and sample documents illustrating major organizational models

■ Summary pages of key skills, such as Conserving Words and Quick Tips for Punctuation

■ Self-assessment activities

■ Sidebars with instructive anecdotes and quotations

Relevant Content

■ Workplace Applications—real documents written by workplace writers from a variety of professions to serve as cases for discussion of the principles of effective writing

■ Before-and-after examples of documents revised by writers like you

■ Writing practice based on workplace scenarios

■ Opportunities for interactive classroom brainstorming (such as, what is your rhetorical purpose and how to generate points for a proposal)

■ Brief introduction to modern letter style

■ Special guidance on electronic communication issues

■ Editing and refining practice on sentences drawn from actual documents

■ Up-to-date rules on workplace preferences in punctuation and mechanics

■ Reader-Friendly Writing Checklist

■ Current list of useful references (e.g., reference manuals, full textbooks on business and technical writing, dictionaries, on-line resources, and specialized topics)

■ Instructor's revision marks and proofreader's marks

Readable Style

■ Plain English explanations

■ Humorous examples

■ An encouraging, coaching "voice"

■ Anecdotes drawn from 25+ years of corporate training experience

On-line Instructor's Manual

An On-line Instructor's Manual supports this book. In it you find methods for using *The Writing Coach* and a philosophy for involving adults in active learning. The old lecture methods just don't work with this audience. When people say, "You made a boring subject interesting," that means they participated and had a good time. The On-line Instructor's Manual describes how to make that involvement happen:

■ Brief presentation of adult learning theory,

■ Methods for involving all class members,

■ Techniques for using the practice exercises in the manual,

■ Analysis of the manual's sample documents,

■ Explanation of how to create customized exercises.

To access the manual, visit our site: <http://www.delmarlearning. com/companions/> and search by author (Johns) or title (*The Writing Coach*). To access all content, enter the user name: johnsolc and password: enter.

COACH—THE AUTHOR

This book has been in process since 1978. That's when I began to teach business and technical writing in corporate classrooms across the United States and abroad. Since then, I have worked with—and learned from—a veritable Who's Who of the American workplace—corporate executives, administrative assistants, geoscientists, bankers, sales and marketing personnel, oil industry field technicians, auditors, university development officers, engineers, accountants, attorneys, computer experts, customer service representatives, city workers, and on and on. From them I learned that the academic models I had been teaching in college did not work in the corporate world; that most bosses (and customers) prefer plain English to a more ornate, literary style; and that time was their most important commodity.

The Writing Coach reflects what I have learned from my clients. It includes models and document samples drawn from many industries. This cross-fertilization has proved useful. Although the content and formats may differ from organization to organization, the needs of readers and the writing process remain pretty much the same. Thus, this book includes what I have gained from many sources in the hopes you will learn from them too.

I have also learned much from my colleagues. My active involvement in several organizations has enriched my professional life—as president and board member of the Association of Professional Communication Consultants, as a workshop leader for the Association for Business Communication, and as a board member of both the American Society of Training and Development and the Association for Women in Communication. In addition, these colleagues have validated my work with awards for instructional design, outstanding training programs, and professional contributions.

Acknowledgments

I am extremely grateful to these "teachers"—clients, seminar participants, and colleagues. In particular, those clients who have allowed me to include their documents in this book deserve our gratitude. Though all individual and organizational names have been changed, being willing to see your documents in print can be both exciting and intimidating. But because the book's relevance depends on its authenticity, the real-world samples are critical. I deeply appreciate my clients' generosity.

The Writing Coach also benefited from the wise editorial eye of many. I often tell seminar participants that "great writers have great editors." Though not claiming greatness, I do credit my colleagues, friends, and reviewers, who have helped me improve this book:

Sherry Scott, director of personnel and training
Citizens Life Insurance
Austin, Texas

Melissa Johns, attorney
Washington, D.C.

Mary Cantrell, assistant professor of English
Tulsa Community College
Tulsa, Oklahoma

Barbara Shwom, past president of the Association for
    Business Communication
The Writing Program and the Kellogg School of
    Management
Northwestern University
Chicago, Illinois

Terri Deems
Worklife Design
Adjunct faculty member—Hamilton College
Ankeny, Iowa

Carol Ann Dennis
Lincoln Technical Institute
Allentown, Pennsylvania

Dena King
Nebraska College of Business
Omaha, Nebraska

Susan J. Klemm
Lincoln School of Commerce
Lincoln, Nebraska

Thanks, too, to Delmar Learning's Pat Gillivan and Nina Tucciarelli for their good advice about content, structure, and design. Cantrell Marketing Group, Tulsa, Oklahoma, created the preliminary graphics. All have been invaluable in developing the final product.

People often ask me, "Who makes these rules?" In a book like this, you should know what authorities I rely on. For all punctuation and mechanics guidance, I refer to *The Gregg Reference Manual,* edited by William Sabin, the best reference for the American workplace. For confirmation, I also consulted Diana Hacker's fine composition text, *A Writer's Reference*, 4th edition, and Martha Kolln's excellent grammar text, *Understanding English Grammar*, 3rd edition. For guidance on word usage and definitions, I used the *American Heritage College Dictionary* and *The New Reading Teacher's Book of Lists* by Edward Bernard Fry, et al. A full list of useful resources appears in Chapter 8, "Fundamentals."

Introduction to The Writing Process

YOUR GOAL: READER-FRIENDLY DOCUMENTS

For too long, business and technical writing has focused on the wrong person—the writer, not the reader. Instead of concentrating on what will make the reader's job easier, professional writing often has emphasized the writer—what language and organization are easiest for him or her. However, to be an effective writer and achieve the results you want, you should write reader-friendly documents: reports, proposals, memos, procedures, letters, and e-mail.

This manual presents strategies to help you make your writing reader-friendly. This term does *not* mean that your ideas are simple or uncomplicated. Often, in professional settings, the ideas to be conveyed are quite complex. But the documents explaining them need not be. To aid, rather than inhibit, your reader's grasp of your ideas, you must have:

- A clear understanding of your audience and purpose for writing.

- A logical organizational plan with a main idea up front to guide your reader.

- A good balance of clearly stated key points and supporting evidence.

- Words that are appropriate and clear to your reader.

- Sentences that are clear and grammatically correct.

- A predictable format that allows your reader to find information easily.

These elements shape The Writing Process, a model for writing clear, complete, and correct documents. This manual follows this process, with each chapter addressing the elements in more detail. Each begins with an overview, followed by explanations, exercises, and samples. Used with permission of the writers and their companies, all samples are real workplace documents representing the kinds of writing people do each day—reporting results, making proposals, transmitting information, solving problems, giving instructions, and corresponding with associates inside and outside their organizations. These samples, especially the original and revised versions, demonstrate the skills achieved by employees who understand how to write reader-friendly documents.

The manual's goal is to help you, too, become a reader-friendly writer.

THE WRITING PROCESS

To use your writing time efficiently, think of writing as a process, not a product. Most of us rarely produce a first-time-perfect document. Instead, we go through a series of steps that lead to the final product—a well-written report, memo, or letter. People's writing processes differ, and individuals vary their practice depending on the type of document and its importance. For most people, the steps even overlap, with organizing running into writing, with some editing along the way. However, you will save time and produce clearer documents if you concentrate on one step at a time as shown in Table 1-1.

Table 1-1. The Writing Process

Stage	Step	What to Do
Prewriting	Planning	• Analyze your audience(s). • Identify your purpose (or reason for writing). • Brainstorm to generate ideas.
	Organizing	• Prepare a blueprint (or outline). • Put main idea up front. • Arrange key points in order. • Identify action wanted.
Writing	Drafting	• Write a draft. • Emphasize key points. • Focus each paragraph. • Impose a clear order.
Rewriting	Editing	• Evaluate clarity and precision of words. • Eliminate unnecessary words. • Tighten sentences.
	Refining	• Correct errors in grammar, punctuation, mechanics, and spelling. • Format text.

Self-Assessment Activity

Analyze your own writing practices. If you are creating a significant document (not a brief note or routine form), what percentage of your writing time do you spend:

Prewriting _____

Writing _____

Rewriting _____

The Case for Managing the Writing Process

Many people cut short one or more steps, thinking "I don't have time to plan, so I'll just start writing." Or they are quick to finish, thinking, "That's good enough. It's just an e-mail, so I don't need to proofread."

The problem is that short-cutting a stage in the writing process often wastes time. Without a good map or blueprint to direct your writing, ideas wander. Such drafts either bury the main idea and key points where the reader won't find them, or they require extensive (and inefficient) reconstruction during the rewriting stage. Similarly, stopping to edit while you write a draft means that your mind is multitasking—trying to balance what you want to say and how you want to say it at the same time. Then if you skimp on proofreading, you risk looking careless—with your written product and perhaps your other work products.

One study of a professional writer revealed this use of the writer's time:

Prewriting	40 percent
Writing	20 percent
Rewriting	40 percent

Professional writers say the art of writing is rewriting—where you achieve the fine polish of great writing. But most workplace writers do not need to spend that much time polishing. There is a "good enough" point at which you need to send the document. However, really important documents may require a high degree of revision. More important, all documents deserve significant planning and organizing before the writing begins.

> People often say, "I don't have time to plan." But if you want to become a reader-friendly writer, you don't have time NOT to plan.

Planning

Potential Problems	Strategies
Document does not focus on readers' needs.	Analyze all your potential readers: ■ What do they know? ■ What do they need to know? ■ What vocabulary are they familiar with?
Readers wonder, "Why am I reading this?"	Ask yourself, "Why am I writing?" Then tell your readers up front. Think about how and when your readers will use the document. Plan a format that makes the information easily accessible.
Most prominent ideas are stale, or important ideas are buried.	Use brainstorming techniques to discover your best ideas—*before* you write.

Planning

CHAPTER 2—PLANNING

PLANNING THE DOCUMENT

Here's the great news: In workplace writing you have real audiences and you write for real purposes. No more inventing an audience and topic or writing just for a grade. But that reality means you need to plan your document to meet your readers' needs and to achieve your purpose—if you want it to succeed.

During prewriting, you face five basic decisions that help shape your writing strategy. These decisions lay the foundation for choosing content, shaping an organizational blueprint, determining an appropriate style, and even designing the document's format. The decisions are:

- Who are my audiences?

- What is my purpose?

- What is my main idea?

- What are my key points?

- What is the action I want?

Planning Decisions

The first two are the planning decisions discussed in this chapter. They are critically important because they determine content, style, and format. Unfortunately, writers often jump directly to "What do I want to say?" (content) without first answering these foundational questions—"to whom?" and "why?"—that analyze the context in which they are writing.

Decision One—Who are my audiences?

- Who will read what I am writing?

- How many different readers are there, and are their needs the same?

- What do the readers expect from my document?

- What information do they need?

- What information do they not need?

- What technical language do we share?

- How receptive are the readers to my message? Hostile? Sympathetic? Neutral?

- Who will do what I want done? Make the decision? Solve the problem?

Decision Two—What is my purpose?

- Why am I writing?

- Is it primarily an informational or a persuasive document?

- How will readers use the document?

- Do different sections have different purposes?

- How should I state why I am writing?

Organizing Decisions

The other three decisions—which identify the main idea, key points, and action—are discussed in Chapter 3, "Organizing," and Chapter 4, "Writing."

DECISION ONE: WHO ARE YOUR AUDIENCES?

First, answer this central question: "Who will read this document?" It is very difficult to write reader-friendly documents without an answer. You can use several techniques to analyze your readers.

Approach One: Analyzing Reader Interest

This approach looks at what information your readers want to know and what vocabulary they share with you.

	These Readers Want to Know:	*In What Style?*
Lay Readers —anyone outside your field	The big picture; general issues and details; "What's in it for me?" (WIIFM) They do not want technical detail.	Plain English
Management —anyone who has oversight responsibilities	The big picture, with particular focus on financial issues: What's it going to cost and what will be the return on investment? They want to know, "What's in it for the company?" (WIIFC)	Plain English

> "I don't want to know how the watch was made. I just want to know what to do with it."
> —A Company President

	These Readers Want to Know:	*In What Style?*
Experts —your professional peers	All the technical details. They may need your document to do their own work. They also will be checking to see whether they agree with your analysis.	Technical language (jargon) is clear, precise, and concise for these readers.
Technicians —people who will do the hands-on work	Some of the technical details, particularly those related to "how to" and "why." They do not want to know everything you know.	Plain English and some jargon.

Approach Two: Analyzing Audience Importance

This method analyzes different readers' uses of your document and which readers are most important to target.

Readers	*What They Will Do with Your Document*
Primary	The reader(s) who will do what you want done: make the decision, solve the problem, follow the procedure, answer your question. If you have to choose whose needs to meet, you should choose the primary reader(s).
Secondary	The readers who will receive your document for information only. At some point, they may use your document, but right now you are only keeping them informed.
Intermediary	The readers who will review your document before it reaches your primary reader(s). They may include your supervisor, an administrative assistant, a manager, your client contacts who will pass the document on to their decision makers. These readers/reviewers have real power over your document, but they are not the decision makers.

Don't make false assumptions:

- That your readers will read the entire document. Many won't.
- That the addressee and the primary audience are the same. Often, the addressee is your pipeline to the primary reader.

Approach Three: Analyzing Your Audience's Expertise

A third way to analyze the complexity of your audiences is to think about who shares your expertise. You will have readers who share some of your knowledge about your organization, the project, and your profession; only those inside the circles' overlap will share all of it.

Figure 2-1 shows who might read a proposal to improve a current product. Assume that a sales representative for Worldwide Widget is writing the proposal because she continued to hear complaints from customers about the reliability of their most recent product. Although customers like the product, they have discovered some potential safety problems that can easily be solved with minor engineering modifications. The sales representative's audience analysis might look like Figure 2-1.

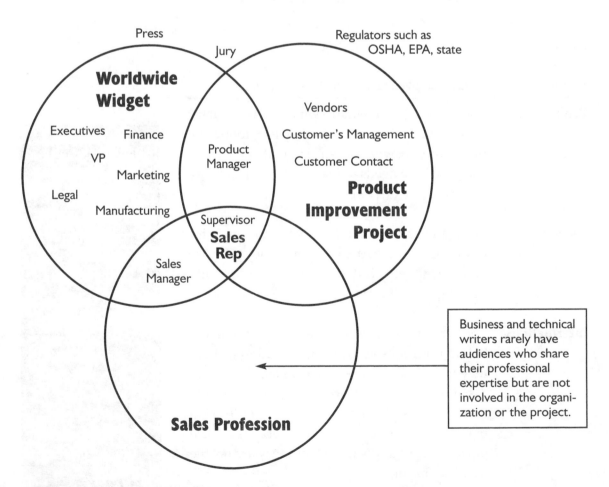

Figure 2-1. The circles of audience expertise

The sales representative's proposal could be read by all these audiences:

- **Primary**—vice president, company engineering and manufacturing departments

- **Intermediaries**—coworkers, supervisor, sales and product managers

- **Secondary**—executives, company legal and finance departments, customer contact and management, vendors

- Possible but not likely—regulators, press, and jury

Audience Worksheet

Answer the following questions by listing either names or categories of your own readers. If you are a student, assume that you have a new job as an office manager and be creative: Make up names and titles. If you are currently working, analyze your actual audiences.

Who normally reads what I write?

Who else might see what I write, both internal and external readers?

Although unlikely, if something goes wrong, who else might read what I write?

> **Remember: The question is not "To whom do I write?" The question is "Who might read what I write?"**

Planning

Practice: Audience Analysis

If you were writing a proposal to purchase new computers and printers for your work group, who might read your proposal?

Using your list from the Audience Worksheet, place the readers of your proposal in their appropriate circles in Figure 2-2 based on how they relate to your organization, the project, and your profession. Notice where your expertise overlaps with your different readers' knowledge. Also think about the routes your documents take to reach these different readers.

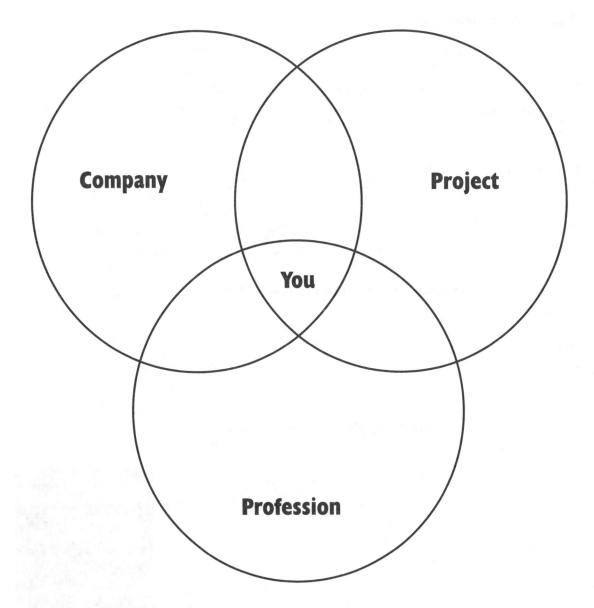

Figure 2-2. Your circles of audience expertise

Workplace Application—Audience Analysis

The audience-unfriendly memo shown in Figure 2-3 was actually sent to people working for this manager. How do you think the readers will react? What results do you think the manager wants? Will the memo achieve those results? If not, why? What would you change?

Practice: Rewrite the memo in Figure 2-3 to focus on meeting the readers' needs for clear content, focus, and appropriate tone. You may add or delete content. (Use the Workspace on page 14.)

Date: May 1, 200_
To: Department Personnel
From: Manager
Subject: Vacation and Work Break Policies

I have noticed in recent weeks a lack of understanding regarding this department's vacation policy. To clarify this matter, I strongly suggest the following guidelines be adhered to:

1) Vacations should be taken only when absolutely necessary. Do not take a week's vacation simply to get away from the company. (If you need to be away from the company that badly, you are probably ready for a change of jobs.)

2) Vacations should be scheduled so as to cause the least negative effect to the company. Plan your work well in advance and leave no loose ends when you do go on vacation.

3) Although the company has granted you two weeks' vacation, do not feel compelled to use the entire two weeks. Unexpected emergencies such as illness or a death in your immediate family, could well put you in a negative position for next year's vacation.

4) Before deciding to use your vacation, you should request counseling time with me. In many cases, sensible discussion will help avoid unpleasant situations later on.

If you have any questions on any of these guidelines, I will be more than happy to discuss them with you.

Due to the length of this memo, work break policies will be addressed in a subsequent memo.

Figure 2-3. Audience-unfriendly memo

WORKSPACE

DECISION TWO: WHAT IS YOUR PURPOSE?

Why Am I Writing?

Writers often confuse their business purpose (or the problem to be solved) with their writing purpose. The business purpose is the issue they are addressing; the writing purpose is why they are writing the document. If they focus only on the business purpose, they easily fall into the trap of telling the story of what happened. Readers usually want to know what you *learned*, not what you *did*.

In planning, you should think about both the business purpose and the writing purpose. Both will usually appear in your first paragraph, and the writing purpose often states the main idea (see Figure 2-4).

Two very general purposes—to inform and to persuade—cover all documents. However, analyzing your purpose more specifically will help you focus the document. For example, a procedure is obviously written to inform. But you will write a better procedure if you identify its purpose as to teach or instruct.

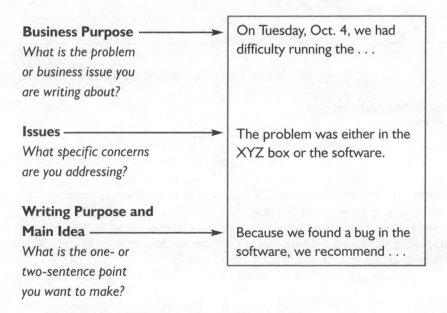

Business Purpose
*What is the problem
or business issue you
are writing about?*

On Tuesday, Oct. 4, we had difficulty running the . . .

Issues
*What specific concerns
are you addressing?*

The problem was either in the XYZ box or the software.

**Writing Purpose and
Main Idea**
*What is the one- or
two-sentence point
you want to make?*

Because we found a bug in the software, we recommend . . .

FIGURE 2-4. Targeting your purpose

Exercise: List five more specific reasons (purposes) for writing documents:

1. _____

2. _____

3. _____

4. _____

5. _____

(See a list of possible purposes on page 19.)

Workplace Application—Analyzing Audience and Purpose

For the product evaluation in Figure 2-5, analyze the writer's sensitivity to his audience and purpose. As you read this first page of a four-page software evaluation, think about how he meets his readers' needs. Who do you think his readers are? What is his writing purpose? What else might he do to make this long document reader-friendly?

Author: I.S. Analyst   Composed: 07/11 11:41 AM

Subject: Computer Master Management as a
          Development Tool

- -

Overview

Computer Master Management is marketed as an end-user relational database management system and reporting tool, but it has features that (many people believe) place it nearly in competition with professional Client/Server development tools such as ProPower. This paper will examine Management as a development environment and attempt to identify the situations where its use is appropriate (and where not).

(continued)

Figure 2-5. Analyzing audience and purpose

What Makes Management So Attractive?

Management was designed as an end-user tool. It is far more easily mastered than any of the current crop of "professional application" development tools. Raw development productivity, especially at first, is easily an order of magnitude faster with Management than with a professional tool such as ProPower.

Other features are:

- Being a Computer Master product with a huge installed base of users, Management is far more stable than most development tools.

- Management's script language is Visual Basic, which is an easy-to-learn language that many people already know.

- User interface windows can be rapidly created by simply specifying a database table, and the windows are strung together to build applications through the use of "Macros." Many applications can be built without writing any code.

- The report writer is extremely powerful and easy to use—it makes the report writers that are bundled with most development tools look primitive in comparison.

- Connections are provided to enterprise-level databases such as Supercompute, which allow these databases to be manipulated in the same ways that local Management databases are manipulated. This makes it possible to use Management as a development tool for enterprise databases.

So Why Not Use Management for Everything?

Management has the potential to someday be grown by Computer Master into a professional development tool that would compete directly with ProPower. But right now, Management is not yet an industrial-strength application development tool:

- Management source code is stored in a Management database, rather than ASCII files. Version control options are extremely limited and entirely Management-specific. One such third-party product is known to exist: "Management Monitor."

- Team development is very difficult, for the same reason. Externally, a Management program looks like a single, monolithic DBS file. Although you can place that file on a LAN server and share it, all the developers have write access and can easily destroy each other's work.

[The report continued for three more pages and ended with . . .]

Summary

Management is an extremely powerful and valuable tool for end-users and a few classes of professionally developed applications. It is not an appropriate choice for the types of industrial-quality applications that I.S. is usually concerned with building.

I.S. should develop the expertise to support the product and should encourage (and manage) its use among the user community. Some means must be found to manage the expectations that Management generates.

Figure 2-5. Analyzing audience and purpose *(concluded)*

Your Analysis

■ Who do you think his readers are?

■ What does he do to meet his readers' needs?

■ What is his writing purpose?

■ What else might he do to make this long document reader-friendly?

Purposes for Writing
(from Targeting Your Purpose exercise)

Persuasive	*Informative*
Your purpose is persuasive if you want your readers to do something: approve your proposal, buy your product, agree with you, follow your instructions. Most workplace writing involves some form of persuasion.	Your purpose is informative if you are simply conveying information that readers need.

Persuasive	Informative
Analyze	Announce
Criticize	Answer
Demand	Ask
Deny	Confirm
Discuss	Congratulate
Entertain	Document
Explain	Inform
Instruct/Teach	Invite
Justify	Thank
Praise	Transmit
Propose	Update
Recommend	
Report	Others?
Request	
Sell	
Suggest	
Others?	

Obviously, some of these purposes sound negative. It's always important to know your purpose. Then you decide how to state it.

Practice: Revising to Clarify Purpose

Revise the memo to John Legal (Figure 2-6) by focusing clearly on its purpose. Why is the writer sending this second request? (The first memo must not have been clear either.) Based on the purpose you identify, rewrite it to state that purpose and clarify the content for the reader. Then compare yours to the writer's revised version in Chapter 7 "Practice," page 222.

Planning

INTEROFFICE CORRESPONDENCE

Date: November 27, 200_
To: John Legal
From: Alice Accounting
Subject: APEX LABORATORIES (Second Request)

The work performed on the above contract was started before the contract was executed; thus it is required that the authority to do this be appropriately documented. Please send this to my attention so that I can attach it to the contract.

This contract is over $50,000, and because of the changes made on this standard form, a preexecution review by the Legal Department should have been completed and documented on or with the contract. Because this contract is for $100,000, insurance verification is required.

If you have any questions, my extension is 5436.

cc: Contract File

Figure 2-6. Revising to clarify purpose

WORKSPACE

BRAINSTORMING TO GENERATE IDEAS

What Might I Want to Say?

Many people start writing to discover what they want to say. That freewriting technique is useful if you need to discover a topic, but most workplace writers already know what they need to write about. With freewriting, you risk getting locked into an organizational structure too early in the writing process. As a result, obvious ideas are up front, your fresh ideas and key points are buried, and revision requires a lot of frustrating reconstruction time.

You can avoid these problems by using brainstorming techniques to generate ideas. Instead of writing full sentences and paragraphs, use these mind-opening strategies to discover your best ideas—*before* you write.

When brainstorming, use phrases in a laundry list if you are a word person, or draw a diagram if you are a picture person. Use any medium to brainstorm: scratch paper, butcher paper, the computer, post-its on a wall. The point is to generate a free flow of ideas before you begin to decide which ones to include in the focused, logically ordered blueprint of your document. Chapter 3, "Organizing," presents an organizational blueprint for each of these idea generators.

Using Words

For proposals	List Pros and Cons for what you are proposing.
For justifications or explanations	Jot down the Point and Reasons.
For informational documents	List the 5 Ws and H: Who, What, When, Where, Why, and How.
For problem-solving documents	Identify . . . • the Problem • the Solution • the Action you want
For procedures	List

The Actor	The Act

Using Diagrams

People who visualize information, including many technically oriented writers, find that drawing a diagram of their main idea and key points is useful. One scientist said she did not know what she was going to say until she laid out all the information on a large piece of butcher paper on a conference room table. Then she could decide which information went in which place in the report. If you prefer a picture to see how things are put together, try these brainstorming techniques.

Draw a cluster of key points and related details:

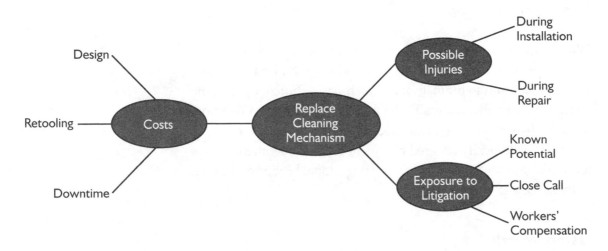

Figure 2-7. Clustering ideas

Or draw a flow chart:

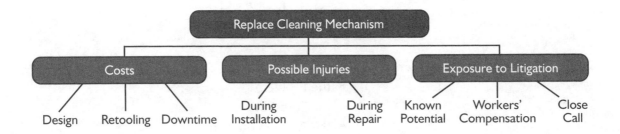

Figure 2-8. Charting ideas

The brainstorming technique you use is not important. But it is important that you generate ideas early, without judging them or worrying about organization or style. In the organizing stage, you will make the decisions about what content to keep, what to eliminate, and what order to arrange your points.

Organizing

Potential Problems	Strategies
Document is a story of what the writer did, with the main idea and key points buried.	Outline your main idea, key points, and support using the ideas and details generated during brainstorming.
Conclusions and recommendations are buried.	Distill the most important points to put in an Overview up front.
Reader gets lost because the document lacks logical order or the order is not apparent.	Use formatting techniques (headings, white space) to highlight your logical progression.

CHAPTER 3—ORGANIZING

ORGANIZING THE DOCUMENT

According to the great Yankees catcher Yogi Berra, "If you don't know where you are going, you might wind up someplace else." How will readers be able to follow your message if you don't know where you are going yourself?

If your goal is to create documents that are reader-friendly, information must be logically arranged and packaged for easy access by readers. In a sense, good organization creates a map for your readers by telling them the main idea of the document (your information destination), the major key points along the way, and the response you need from them when they reach the destination. Like a well-drawn map, a well-organized document is predictable.

You focus your readers' expectations by:

■ Including an Overview at the beginning of longer documents;

■ Using point-first structures: main idea in the first paragraph and key points at the beginning of body paragraphs;

■ Using content-oriented headings throughout the document;

■ Breaking up heavy text with white space, headings, columns, and **bold** key terms;

■ Substituting graphics and meaningful captions for text, when appropriate.

During planning, you identified your audiences and targeted your purpose. This chapter covers the organizing decisions that complete the Prewriting Stage:

Decision Three—What is my main idea?
If I could write only one sentence to make my point, what would I say?

Decision Four—What are my key points?
If I could explain briefly, in only a few sentences, what would I say?

Decision Five—What is the action I want?
What do I want the reader(s) to do?

The answers to these questions form the map that guides your readers through all documents—from very long reports, to proposals, to shorter memoranda, letters, and e-mail. The central question is, "How can I organize information to make the reader's job as easy as possible?"

THE PROCESS: DRAWING THE MAP

From your brainstormed ideas generated during planning, you are now ready to make decisions about content and order.

First, review your material:

■ Identify your key points by grouping related items and giving them a label—for example, everything related to *costs*, everything related to *efficiency*, everything related to *schedule*, and so forth.

■ Drop items that are not relevant to this audience and purpose, even though they may be true. What is important to you may not be that important to your readers.

■ Look for content gaps. Have you overlooked any significant details? Do you need to gather more information to support some points?

Second, based on your audience analysis, arrange your key points in descending order of importance to your primary audience(s). In workplace writing, this order often moves from quantifiable issues (e.g., cost, productivity) to softer issues (e.g., image, morale). Other methods of logical arrangement are outlined in Chapter 4, "Writing."

Finally, write a working main idea. Although you write it last, it will appear in the first paragraph of your document to guide your readers. In a sense, the main idea is a contract you make with your readers, promising to give them certain information in a certain order. At this point it is only a working draft; you may revise it during editing.

Organizing

ORGANIZING SHORTER DOCUMENTS

You should have an overall map or blueprint for organizing your ideas in shorter documents (one to two pages) or in the discussion sections of longer documents. Although the next chapter on writing paragraphs goes into more detail (just as you do when you plan each paragraph), the diagram in Figure 3-1 helps you visualize how the parts of a one- to two-page document fit together. It also turns the brainstorming from Planning into a clearly organized document blueprint.

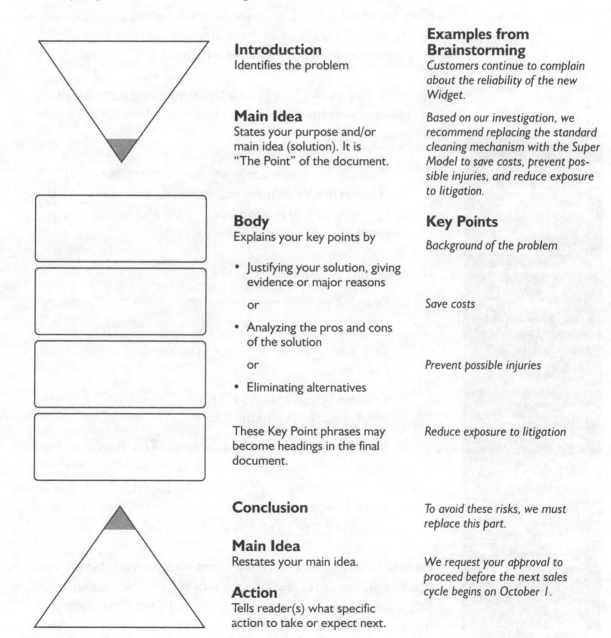

Introduction
Identifies the problem

Main Idea
States your purpose and/or main idea (solution). It is "The Point" of the document.

Body
Explains your key points by

• Justifying your solution, giving evidence or major reasons

  or

• Analyzing the pros and cons of the solution

  or

• Eliminating alternatives

These Key Point phrases may become headings in the final document.

Conclusion

Main Idea
Restates your main idea.

Action
Tells reader(s) what specific action to take or expect next.

Examples from Brainstorming
Customers continue to complain about the reliability of the new Widget.

Based on our investigation, we recommend replacing the standard cleaning mechanism with the Super Model to save costs, prevent possible injuries, and reduce exposure to litigation.

Key Points
Background of the problem

Save costs

Prevent possible injuries

Reduce exposure to litigation

To avoid these risks, we must replace this part.

We request your approval to proceed before the next sales cycle begins on October 1.

Figure 3-1. Organizing short documents

DECISION THREE:
WHAT IS MY MAIN IDEA?

Your main idea is the point you are trying to make. It is the answer to the question, "If I could write only one sentence and it couldn't be long, what would I say?"

In a short memo, letter, or e-mail, one sentence should clearly and concisely state your most important message. In long reports, the Conclusions and Recommendations in the Overview component cover the main idea. If your document does not take a position (as in a request for information or answers to several questions), the statement of purpose replaces a main idea.

The main idea *should* state your judgment on the subject you are addressing. Sometimes it also briefly summarizes the key points to follow:

> Despite the initial cost, we recommend purchasing the XYZ equipment to reduce on-going operational and maintenance costs and to improve departmental efficiency. ← Main Idea Key Point Summary

The main idea *should not*:

1. Be incomplete. It must be a sentence that clearly conveys the point of your document.

2. Be a question. Do not force your readers to guess your main idea.

3. Contain hedgers such as "I think." If you make the statement, you obviously think it.

4. Be vague or garbled. For example, "This issue has some significant ramifications for the economic situation of the corporation" does not say anything. Get to the point. Be clear: "To prevent further loss of market share, we must increase our sales efforts immediately."

Having a clear main idea is important both for you and for your readers. In the organizing stage, writing a working main idea helps you clarify and control your ideas. In the final document, the refined main idea tells your readers your point up front. They should not have to search for your destination or fit the pieces together as they read.

Your subject line has high priority.

The subject line is critical in attracting readers' attention, especially in e-mail. A good subject line contains your reduced main idea, not just the general topic you are addressing. It also permits efficient retrieval if readers need to find your document in a file. Therefore,

Instead of
Subject: Brochure Copy

Write
Subject: Approval of Brochure Copy Needed by Oct. 1

DECISION FOUR:
WHAT ARE MY KEY POINTS?

Each paragraph in your document should make a key point that helps advance your main idea. In organizing your overall document, you identify the key points and arrange them in logical order. Your readers expect to find the key point at the beginning of each body paragraph, followed by details or further explanation. Chapter 4, "Writing," focuses on how to write clear, effective paragraphs that support your key points.

Workplace Application—
Analyzing a Good Memo

The entertaining memo shown in Figure 3-2 was widely read and remembered for several reasons. Think about what you like about it; identify the main idea, key points, and action.

From: Susan Smiley
To: All Employees
Subject: Use of Conference Room Space
Date: Wednesday, June 21, 200_, 10:28 a.m.

We continue to have a problem with what one might term "conference room terrorists," i.e., people who have a tendency to engage in the following search and destroy tactics:

- Assume they can commandeer conference room space without checking to see if the space has already been reserved;

- Don't adhere to the schedule and don't evacuate the room when time is up (this is why there are so many nose prints on the glass windows . . .);

- Book space, decide on a different mission, and then disappear into the jungle without canceling the space;

- Use a conference room for two or three commandos when an office or workstation would serve the same purpose;

- Seize the space reserved by someone else without proper advance warning.

I'm attempting a somewhat humorous (that remains to be seen, I guess) approach to an enemy which has plagued us for years—lack of conference space. You would think that with 15 conference rooms, we could find a place to gather the troops peacefully.

(continued)

Figure 3-2. Analyzing a good memo

There are always extenuating circumstances which force all of us to be flexible from time to time—special meetings which arise suddenly, unexpected visitors, lots of people decided that they just HAD to go to YOUR meeting, and you didn't plan enough space—the list goes on and on. HOWEVER, practice basic courtesy with your fellow employees; I would hate to have to go out on a search-and-rescue mission after you don't . . . I prefer to use words as my weapon of choice.

Use the conference room scheduler. It's a great device—even I know how to use it, believe it or not. If I can, just about anyone who knows how to turn on the PC can. It's possible that we can make some refinements to this system to help you even more. It's a secret operation—don't call Linda or Jane; they don't know yet, either. We'll keep you posted.

Along other lines, all conference rooms will no longer be available for use by any employee or outsider for any profit-making purpose, regardless of whether such meeting might be at noon or after hours and even if these rooms aren't being used by anyone else for business reasons. Conference rooms can be reserved to host group meetings for professional organizations of which employees are members, and they will continue to be available for any employee-related function, such as birthday celebrations, wedding/baby showers, going-away parties, etc. Use the regular conference room scheduler for these events. The only codicil: if the room is required for a business purpose, that takes precedence over any non-business reason, but use the same guidelines discussed above!

If you have any questions as to whether or not your particular purpose meets the criteria, please contact the HR Department. We'll be wearing our regulation flak jackets.

Figure 3-2. Analyzing a good memo *(concluded)*

Workplace Application— Reorganizing for Clarity

The e-mail in Figure 3-3, sent to managers to enlist their help in orienting their new employees, was routinely ignored. The original e-mail content focused on giving *information* about the Human Resource (HR) Department's program and what HR needed from the manager. In the revised version, the writer saw his purpose as *persuasive*: Here is what HR needs to help the manager and the bank successfully orient the new employee and reduce employee turnover.

In analyzing the original, answer these questions:

- What is the main idea and where do you find it?

- What are the key points?

- What is the manager supposed to do?

Starting recently, the Human Resource Department has implemented a new all day (8:30–4:30) orientation process to assist in reducing the bank's turnover. Included in the new program is the involvement of managers and regional managers. We will be serving lunch between 11:30 a.m. through 12:30 p.m. and would like all managers, available to attend, to join their new employee for lunch in the Bank Café. **(If you are available to attend please meet in the Human Resources office at 11:25; also, please remember to wear your name tags.) Please notify me of your availability as soon as possible.**

To ensure accuracy on all new hires, please complete the following forms for new employees:

- Survey of Applicant Quality

- Supervisor Checklist

Upon completion, please route to the attention of H.R. Jones at mail stop 1.3. For all supervisors' convenience I also enclosed a "New Hire Information" Worksheet. This provides management with the resources needed for obtaining system access. If any additional information is needed or if you have a scheduling problem for lunch, please contact me at my extension listed below.

Please remember to obtain the computer System Request Form, schedule the appropriate training and companywide orientation.

Thank you,

H. R. Jones

City Bank, N.A.
Human Resource Assistant
(566) 555-5555

Figure 3-3. Original e-mail

Notice how the order of key points and the format change in the revised version (Figure 3-4). Answer the same questions:

- ▪ What is the main idea and where do you find it?

- ▪ What are the key points?

- ▪ What is the manager supposed to do? Notice how easy the action will be.

The Human Resource Department has implemented a new, all-day (8:30–4:30) orientation process to assist in reducing the bank's turnover. If you are a manager involved with completing paperwork and orientating new employee(s), your participation is needed in several ways:

- **Free food!** Who can pass this up?! To involve the managers, we are providing lunch in the Bank Café on orientation day. You are encouraged to attend with your new employee(s) and meet in the Human Resources office at 11:25 a.m. If you plan to attend, please RSVP by the Thursday prior to orientation. *(Please remember to wear your name tags for those of us that are forgetful!)*

- **To ensure accuracy on all new hires, please complete the following for new employees:**

  1. Please submit a **"System Request Form"** on all new employees to set up their user profiles. The attached link will direct you to Data Security's home page. Select the appropriate System Request Form for your department, fill in the appropriate information and click "Submit".

     (http://www. exchange.com)
     For your convenience I have also attached a **"New Hire Information"** worksheet (the attached file name is: employee's last name, first name_id.doc). This gives you the resources you need to complete the System Request Form properly and thoroughly.

     <<Sampson, Susan_M022221.doc>>

  2. Supervisor Checklist
     <<Supervisor checklist.doc>> *Due Friday following orientation*

  3. Survey of Applicant Quality
     <<Applicant Quality Survey.doc>> *Due Friday following orientation*

Please send the Supervisor Checklist and the Survey of Applicant Quality to H. R. Jones at mail stop 1.3 or e-mail to hrjones@bank.com.

If I can help or if you have a scheduling problem for lunch, please call me at my extension listed below. Your support is greatly appreciated.

H. R. Jones

Human Resources Representative
City Bank N. A.
566-555-5555

Figure 3-4. Revised e-mail

Practice: Reorganizing a Memorandum

The memorandum in Figure 3-5 lacks clear focus. It covers most (not all) of the relevant information, but focuses on what the contest is, not on what might appeal to art instructors. The memo is not wrong; it just will not generate much enthusiasm. Your assignment is to transform it from "adequate" to "excellent."

Develop a blueprint for a new memo that is more persuasive. First think about the specific purpose of the memo. Then, what would art instructors want to know and what would motivate them to have students participate in the contest? Who else might read the memo? Brainstorm possible content. Then, in the workspace on the next page, create a blueprint for the memo using traditional outline form, the diagram model for short documents, clusters, or a flow chart. Do *not* rewrite the original memo. The point is to practice organizing before you write full sentences and paragraphs.

MEMORANDUM

TO: Art Instructors
FROM: Executive Director
SUBJECT: Youth Art Contest
DATE: April 17, 200_

Enclosed is information about a youth art contest Outdoor Boys and Girls is sponsoring in connection with our spring fundraiser, JUST PLANE FUN.

We're looking for entries from boys and girls in Kindergarten through 12th grade. As indicated, the theme is aviation—to correspond to the theme of our fundraiser.

All entries will be displayed at the event on Saturday, June 3, at the Aviation Jet Center at Brookside Airport. Winners will be selected by popular vote from the attending guests.

JUST PLANE FUN generates income that helps pay program fees for boys and girls whose families might not be able to afford participation in Outdoor programs. The contest offers a way for adults attending the fundraiser to connect with youth.

Don't hesitate to contact us if you have any questions or need more information.

Figure 3-5. Reorganizing a memorandum

PREWRITING WORKSPACE

DECISION FIVE:
WHAT IS THE ACTION I WANT?

Readers are often frustrated by documents that make them wade through explanation to find the answer to "What am I supposed to do?" The easy response form in Figure 3-6 meets readers' needs by:

■ Putting the request for action up front;

■ Making the readers' choices clear with a visual layout;

■ Delaying the background to the end as an explanatory footnote.

These days, effective workplace writers are building in their response form at the end of a standard memo or letter. If the document is easy to return or fax, writers are more likely to get a quick response. E-mail programs also permit an immediate response, so building your action item into the text allows your readers to respond promptly (see revised e-mail in Figure 3-4).

PAYER'S REQUEST FOR TAXPAYER IDENTIFICATION NUMBER

Please complete this questionnaire (all 3 items) and return it in the enclosed envelope as soon as possible.

1. Nature of your business with Pipe Line Company (CHECK ONLY ONE):

    [ ]   Provide **services** (even though some goods may be provided)
    [ ]   Provide **goods** (even though some services may be provided)
    [ ]   **Rent** property, equipment or right-of-way
    [ ]   Provide **medical** or health care services
    [ ]   Provide **legal** services
    [ ]   Received payment for **damages**
    [ ]   Other (explain) _____

2. Please CHECK ONLY ONE in either A or B:

    A. Generally exempt from information reporting because my company is:

    [ ] Corporation   [ ] Pipe Line Company
    [ ] Tax Exempt Organization   [ ] Governmental Agency

    ———————————————— OR ————————————————

    B. Not exempt from information reporting because I am:

    [ ] Individual or Sole Proprietorship
    [ ] Partnership

3. Taxpayer Identification Number (TIN):
    (COMPLETE ONLY ONE BOX BELOW)

    Taxpayer Identification Number

    _ _ - _ _ _ _ _ _ _

        OR

    Social Security Number

    _ _ _ - _ _ - _ _ _ _

    Signature _____ Date_____

    NOTE: The U.S. Internal Revenue Code requires us to report payments we have made for services. We are required to include the Payee's TIN on Form 1099. You are required by law to provide us with your correct Taxpayer Identification Number. If you do not provide us with your correct number, you may be subject to civil or criminal penalties imposed by law. The Tax Compliance Act of 1983 requires us to withhold 20% of payment reportable on Form 1099 unless the Payee's correct TIN has been furnished.

Figure 3-6. Making action easy

Organizing

ORGANIZING LONGER DOCUMENTS

Long documents, those of more than two pages, can be particularly challenging to write for several reasons:

■ They are *long* and, therefore, require time for the writer *and* the reader.

■ They are usually not written at one sitting, so it is easy for the writer to lose focus.

■ They can often be the result of a team project, thus having multiple authors and reviewers, with different opinions about content and different styles.

■ Readers probably will not read them all at one time. In fact, many readers will read only part of the document, not the whole.

■ They can be very important, carrying high stakes and a long shelf life.

Long documents require an organizational strategy that allows you to efficiently manage both the writing and the document review process. Your strategy should also produce a document that gives readers a clear map up front and allows easy access to the information they need.

Figure 3-7 presents a reader-friendly model for longer documents. It and the report format that follows were developed for a scientific research report. Not only are they useful for all types of technical documents, but they also work well for organizing feasibility studies, product evaluations, engineering plans, long proposals, audit reports, workforce analyses—in other words, any complex document with multiple sections.

The model in Figure 3-7 is based on these assumptions:

■ Writers work from bottom to top. First they collect all the data that is documented in the Appendix. Then they choose the most important information to analyze in the Discussion. Finally, they write the Overview, which contains the conclusions and recommendations—the big picture.

■ Readers work from top to bottom, with the size of the audience decreasing as the report becomes more detailed.

■ Different sections of the Discussion may have different audiences and purposes, as outlined in the report format that follows.

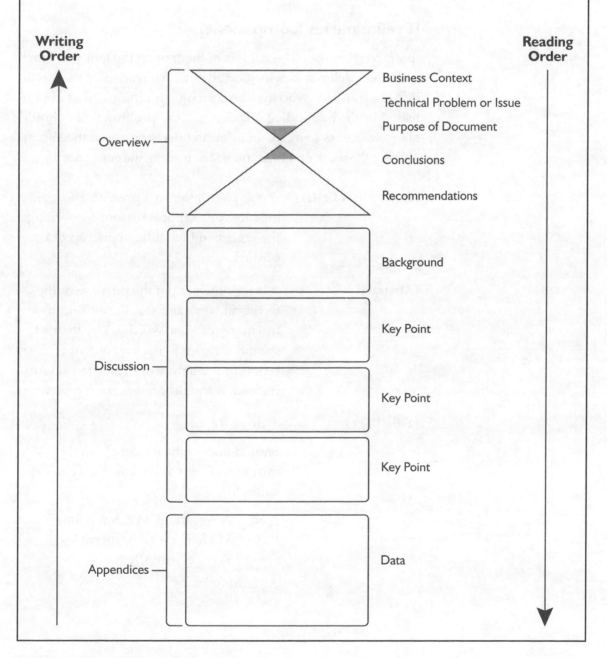

Model for Mapping Longer Documents

Writing Order
We write from bottom to top: Collect all the data, choose the most important to discuss, and then reach conclusions and recommendations.

Reading Order
We read from top to bottom: Readers want to know the big picture in an Overview before they encounter the explanation and details in the Discussion.

Writing Order

Reading Order

Overview
- Business Context
- Technical Problem or Issue
- Purpose of Document
- Conclusions
- Recommendations

Discussion
- Background
- Key Point
- Key Point
- Key Point

Appendices
- Data

Figure 3-7. Mapping longer documents

MODEL REPORT FORMAT

This format is set up in four components: Preliminaries, Overview, Discussion, and Appendix. These distinct sections are designed for different purposes and audiences. Some parts are always needed; others are optional, depending on the content. In this model format, the optional sections are **[bracketed]**. The goal is to provide a useful but *flexible* model for writing longer reports (over two pages).

[Preliminaries Component]

Audience/Purpose: The readers of the transmittal letter, abstract, and other preliminaries include all potential readers of the report, including anyone who may be searching for information in published or on-line indices. Therefore, the preliminaries should allow searchers to make an informed decision about the significance of the work and their interest in reading the entire document.

[Transmittal Letter]	A one-page letter that presents the major business or technical reasons for writing the report and what the report accomplished.
[Abstract]	A brief statement of the purpose of the technical work and significant findings (no more than 250 words). The abstract should *not* merely list the content of the report or the nature of the technical work. Instead, it should present the big picture.
[Title Page]	**Title of Report**
	Should inform the reader about the business benefit as well as the technical subject.

Not: A Report on XYZ Modeling
But: Modeling XYZ to Increase Oil Recovery in ABC

Author(s)
Date

[Table of Contents]   For reports over five pages.

[Lists of Figures and Tables]

Overview Component

Audience/Purpose: The Overview allows general readers (management or lay readers) to grasp the significance of the technical work: The reason it was undertaken, important findings and recommendations, and the benefits to the company and to their groups.

Style: The Overview should be written for a lay audience. Headings should be informative. Use lists of items when appropriate, because white space improves readability.

Business Context	Identifies the business reason for doing this study—the benefits to the organization—and then briefly describes the technical problem you attempted to solve or analyze.
Purpose	Briefly states the purpose of the *report*.
[Objectives]	What *specific* objectives or questions did the study address?
[Methodology]	Briefly outlines the experimental method, *only* if the method itself is critical to understanding the conclusions and recommendations.
Conclusions	Lists the major results and/or conclusions. These can be further developed in the Discussion component.
Recommendations	Lists recommendations for action or next steps by management and/or operations.
Cost Statement	This section *briefly* outlines the cost of the recommended action(s).

To quote one manager, the Overview "should be written in language that anyone, including managers, can understand."

Discussion Component

Audience/Purpose: The Discussion (or Body) of the report develops the ideas presented in the Overview. Written primarily for other technical experts and for informed readers, it allows you to fully explain technical objectives, methodology, findings, and the logic leading to conclusions and recommendations. The Discussion transfers the important technical information to readers who will improve operations. Therefore, it should focus on significant points rather than reporting all data.

Style/Format: Although clarity is still a goal, using technical language (jargon) is appropriate in the Discussion. Adding informative headings and subheadings will help readers grasp the content of each section and will permit easy reference. Clearly focused tables and graphs may be included, but detailed graphics and calculations belong in the Appendix.

The nature of the technical work and the intended audience(s) and purpose should dictate the content of the report and the order for arranging sections. Workplace audiences generally expect to see sections arranged in *decreasing* order of importance or from general to specific. The following list includes *possibilities, not requirements,* of sections in the Discussion.

Possible Sections	*Content*
Problem Statement	What technical problem did the study address?
Specific Technical Questions or Tasks	What were the technical objectives? These may be posed as questions.
Background of the Problem	What was the history leading up to the current study?
[Pertinent Assumptions]	What assumptions limit the applicability of the study?
[Study Background]	What research has been done before?
[Definitions]	What special terms need to be defined so that all readers understand?

Possible Sections	*Content*
Technical Procedure	The description of the procedure should include only information that is necessary to understanding the findings, conclusions, and recommendations. Detailed documentation of the method should appear in the Appendix.
Results or Findings	What were the results of the technical work? How did the findings answer the technical questions posed?
[Cost Analysis]	If the report recommendations require funding, a thorough analysis of current versus future costs is important.
[Schedule]	If a new project will result from the study, identify the chronology of tasks, perhaps in a timeline.
Conclusions	What conclusions have been drawn from the findings? This section elaborates on the list of conclusions in the Overview component.
Recommendations	What actions should be taken based on the conclusions? This section also elaborates on the list of recommendations in the Overview.
[Future Work]	What future work is needed to complete the investigation or what additional questions has the study raised?
[Bibliography/References]	What sources did you consult during the study? What references would the reader(s) need to know about?

Appendix Component

Audience/Purpose: The Appendix documents the entire technical effort. It includes the data and very detailed information of interest primarily to other experts.

Content: The Appendix may include:

- Theory
- Mathematical development
- Equipment
- Experimental or testing procedure
- Literature or patent search
- Data and results
- Site study
- Workpapers
- Detailed graphs, tables, charts, drawings, photographs

Workplace Application— Internal Audit Report

The report in Figure 3-8 applies this report format to a standard workplace document—an internal audit report. Mandated by an innovative manager, the format challenged the traditional audit report formats widely used by internal audit departments. Instead of placing Scope and Objectives (what the auditors looked at during their investigation) and background up front, this report meets the needs of the *primary audiences*: the manager and key individuals who will use the report's recommendations to improve operations. They want to know:

- How are we doing?
- What do we need to change to do better?

Those two questions are answered in the Overview page, and the recommendation comes first in each finding (*Note:* Only one finding out of four has been included). The documentation of the Scope and Objectives (of interest to other auditors as secondary readers) is held until the end of the report, with the courtesies. This report achieves its primary purpose—to recommend four ways to improve operations in the Supply & Distribution and the Wholesale Marketing departments of Petroleum, Inc.—by putting the recommendations up front where management expects them.

Report Overview Component

Confidential—Internal Audit Report

Company	Petroleum, Inc.	**Audit Subject and Location**	Petroleum, Inc.—Supply and Distribution and Wholesale Marketing
Audit No.			Local City, State
Audit Date	August 24, 200_		

Summary Audit Results:

Our audit of the Petroleum, Inc., Supply and Distribution (S&D) and Whole-sale Marketing Departments indicated excellent compliance by both departments to internal and operational controls in the areas of exchange and spot contract administration and documentation, supply forecast and inventory control information systems, and wholesale product pricing. Our review, however, indicated the need for Management attention to: ◄— Conclusion

- Using database software to operate current department information systems more effectively,

- Implementing a refined products quality control program, ◄— Recommendations

- Expanding retail sales forecast procedures, and

- Establishing freight verification procedures.

Mr. _____ and Ms. _____ agreed to the audit comments and recommendations. Mr. _____ indicated that the implementation of improvements relative to quality control, sales forecasting and freight verification procedures would depend on involvement by the Retail Division and the Accounting Department. Presently, the S&D Department has been assigned neither the specific responsibility nor the staff to direct such activities. ◄— Action

Please read and reply as indicated using the response format set out on the reverse side. Forward your reply and other comments to:	GENERAL AUDITOR

Copies or Excerpts to:	Location:	Paragraphs	Reply Required	
CEO	Central, State	All	No	
President	Central, State	All	No	Actions
Division Manager	Local City, State	All	No	
Group Manager	Local City, State	All	Yes	Primary Reader
Audit Manager	Central, State	All	No	
Big Eight Auditor	Central, State	All	No	
Central Files	Central, State	All	No	

Your Copy	Approved by:	Audit Manager		Date:	August 26, 200_

(continued)

Figure 3-8. Internal audit report

Report Discussion Component

TO: Audit Manager   DATE: August 26, 200_

FROM: Auditors

SUBJECT: Petroleum, Inc.   Reference: PE000-00
Supply and Distribution
and Wholesale Marketing of
Finished Product

I.   **Audit Summary**
      Introduction

An internal audit of the Supply and Distribution and Wholesale Marketing Departments of Petroleum, Inc. was performed during the period of June 9 through July 25, 200_. The audit was completed by Tom Smith and Julia Johnson and included three weeks of fieldwork at the Local City Refinery.

The audit scope and objectives are summarized in Section II of this report.

Audit Issues: Control Practices and Procedures

The results of our audit indicated excellent compliance by the two departments, Supply and Distribution and Wholesale Marketing, in carrying out their functions in accordance with Management's directives.

During the first quarter of 200_, the efforts of both departments were plagued significantly by ESI software problems affecting the truck rack reporting system, unfavorable variances in exchange, wholesale, and retail demand, volatile market prices, and the performance of a refinery turnaround. Continuing attention, however, appears to be directed toward each of these areas as well as toward developing integrated strategies of inventory control and marketing.

Audit issues requiring Management's consideration and action noted during the audit were as follows:

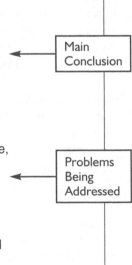

Main Conclusion

Problems Being Addressed

Figure 3-8. Internal audit report *(continued)*

Subject: Supply, Distribution & Marketing   To: Audit Manager
          of Finished Product   Prepared by: Auditors
Audit   Date: August 26, 200_
Ref: PE000-00

Page 2

A. The Supply and Distribution Department should evaluate the feasibility of networking department microcomputers using database software to operate current department information systems more effectively. ← Recommendation

During our audit, we reviewed the Supply and Distribution (S&D) Department's various information systems relating to forecasting, inventory control, and product scheduling. We noted several instances in which the same information is used repeatedly and input to different microcomputers.

Presently, these S&D systems are not integrated, and an information database does not exist. Consequently, all communication of information between staff members must be done manually. The data used at each microcomputer workstation must be input separately into each spreadsheet or report used by that system. ← Problem Identified

In the absence of an integrated system, the potential exists for the following:

- Input error
- Inconsistent information
- Inefficient time usage
- Inadequate response time needed to analyze changes in production or the marketplace ← Potential Effects

Consolidation of data across the functional areas of forecasting, inventory control, and scheduling should improve the quality of information in addition to streamlining information gathering procedures. ← Benefits of Change

Discussion with Management

Since the audit, Group Manager has initiated discussions with a consultant currently contracted to establish database systems for the Transportation Department. Manager has also emphasized input quality control procedures to improve information generated by the present systems. ← Actions Taken

[*The report presented the three additional findings, which have been omitted here. They followed the same structure.*]

(continued)

Figure 3-8. Internal audit report *(continued)*

Subject: Supply, Distribution & Marketing
of Finished Product
Audit
Ref: PE000-00

To: Audit Manager
Prepared by: Auditors
Date: August 26, 200_

Page 4

II.   Audit Scope and Objectives

Our audit scope encompassed supply, distribution, and marketing activities during the twelve months preceding the audit, with particular emphasis on January through May 200_. Also included was a limited review of Petroleum's International spot market transactions.

> Documentation for Other Auditors

The primary objectives of the audit were to assess the reasonable-ness of:

- Supply forecast and inventory control information systems,
- Exchange and spot contract administration and documentation,
- Wholesale product pricing and marketing procedures, and
- Exchange accounting procedures.

III.   Audit Conclusion

A draft copy of the report was reviewed by Manager and Director. General concurrence to the audit recommendations was expressed. To complete the audit process on a timely basis, a written response is requested from Manager by September 26, 200__.

> Action

We wish to express our appreciation to the staff members in both the Supply and Distribution and the Wholesale Marketing Departments as well as in International for the excellent cooperation and assistance we received during our audit.

> Courtesies

_____   _____
Internal Audit Manager   Senior Auditor

_____
Associate Auditor

Figure 3-8. Internal audit report *(concluded)*

Practice: Writing an Overview

The article in Figure 3-9 appeared in the September issue of a public school system's newsletter to taxpayers and system employees. It explains how the superintendent and the school district are handling the continuing budget cuts that threaten to hurt the quality of public school instruction. You will find the major points buried deep in the article, probably reflecting the superintendent's assumption that people will read the entire article (a faulty assumption).With this indirect plan, he risks annoying his audience. A more straightforward approach—overview with big picture up front—would give busy readers the information they want and probably ensure that more people would read the entire article.

For this exercise, based on the superintendent's audience and purpose, go through the process of developing an Overview:

1. Highlight the information that you think should be up front in an Overview. Look for *ideas*, not full sentences.

2. Construct a general map (or outline) for the Overview.

3. Write an Overview for the article that would summarize the major points citizens and employees would want to know.

If you want more practice, use the same article content to prepare an Overview for a report to the school board on the current budget crisis. Would you choose the same information? Would you organize it in the same order? Would the style and format be the same?

Superintendent Explains Difficulty in Setting Year's Operating Budget

Dear Patrons and Employees:

I would like to take this opportunity to extend greetings to you from the office of the superintendent for the first time for this school year. I feel that the new school year offers every indication of being a very excellent one for those most directly involved with the schools, the students and the staff members, and should also provide many satisfying moments for parents as they place the responsibility in the hands of the professional staff members for the education of their youngsters.

(continued)

Figure 3-9. Writing an overview

As has been communicated through the media during the summer months, it was necessary that I make some difficult recommendations to the school board, and for the school board to make some difficult decisions as part of the budgeting process for the school year. Although inflation is proceeding at a rate greater than 13 percent so far during this calendar year, the increases in expenditures for staff, materials and the overall programs within the school system amount to slightly more than 8 percent. This 8 percent increase in expenditures was built into the school year budget, a budget which provides for only a 4.5 percent increase in revenue for the next school year. Obviously, with the revenue falling almost 4 percent below expenditures and almost 8 percent below inflationary cost increases, it will not be possible for this school system next year and, in all likelihood, in years to come, to maintain the same levels of programming and staffing within the school system.

For the most part the more than 150 cuts in this year's budget were made in the non-instructional areas, such as a 37 percent reduction in the custodial force, a 13 percent reduction in the maintenance force, and other total elimination of departments such as the Staff Development Department and the Graphic Arts Department. Further reductions in administrative and administrative-related support personnel have now reduced expenditures in administrative costs within the school system to approximately $750,000.

As we begin our budget planning for next year and the years ahead, it is very obvious that further reductions in expenditures are going to be required. I am very concerned with some of the reductions in instructional program areas which were required to be made for this next year, such as a 50 percent reduction in the number of teacher aides in the schools, the reduction of staff in the Diagnostic Instruction Program and the various other program reductions which had to be made. These are just a preview of more extensive cuts to come in instructional program areas for the years ahead.

As a result of the enrollment decline, I do feel that some further consolidation of staff, programs, and facilities within the school system can be accomplished as we've been doing in the past number of years. However, we cannot continue to make many further reductions in the years ahead without, in my opinion, seriously impairing the instructional programs in the schools.

In addition to spending a considerable portion of my time and effort in the months ahead attempting to identify further areas in which expenditures can be reduced in the school system, I will also be seeking ways of increasing revenue for this school system. City Public Schools simply cannot continue to offer the high level of programming which has been offered in the past many years with such a tremendous gap between inflationary cost increases and revenue increases provided for this school system. Recently you have been hearing of some "victories" for the taxpayers in our county. I would urge that each time you read of such victories, that you first of all pause for a moment and consider whether these victories might not in fact be a defeat for our children in the schools. All of us are concerned about taxes, but, at the same time, all of us should also be concerned about maintaining the same high level of instructional programs in this school system in which we have taken such great pride in the past. To not do so would be a real disservice to our children and to the community as a whole.

The challenges facing this school system—and this entire community—are very real and difficult. But citizens, given the opportunity, have always responded to the educational needs of their children. I feel confident that the combined efforts of citizens who place a high priority on the education of children and the dedicated, professional staff of this school system will result in the ultimate resolution of our common problems.

Best wishes for a successful school year.

John Smith
Superintendent

Figure 3-9. Writing an overview (concluded)

WORKSPACE

Organizing

ORGANIZING YOUR BRAINSTORMED IDEAS

The next pages illustrate how to organize the ideas generated from the brainstorming techniques outlined in Chapter 2, "Planning." These models are useful for organizing all types of documents—proposals, memoranda, letters, e-mail, and procedures.

■ Pros and Cons	For proposals or the benefit/risk section of a longer document.
■ Point and Reasons	For justifications or explanations of why you are suggesting an idea.
■ 5 Ws and H	For purely informational documents such as minutes, trip reports, or meeting announcements.
■ Problem/Solution/ Action	For problem-solving documents of all types. This is a common pattern in all business documents, including the overview of a longer document.
■ Actor/Act	For procedures.

In longer documents, you may use different methods to organize different sections. For example, you would identify pros and cons to brainstorm the benefits versus risks section and the 5 Ws and H for a detailed project schedule.

ORGANIZING A PROPOSAL

There are many right ways to organize a proposal. As in all documents, content and organization are determined by who will read your proposal, who will make the decision, and what is most important to those readers. However, certain guidelines help you plan:

■ If the proposal is lengthy (more than two pages), follow the report format principles that package information in different sections.

■ Always include a brief management summary in plain English up front that includes what you are proposing, benefits (pros) to the "buyer," and the action you are requesting.

▪ Always include the cost, preferably early in the proposal. That's the information your readers are looking for.

▪ Based on your brainstormed pros and cons, make concessions or address risks to establish your credibility. If possible, offset each concession with a pro.

▪ Remember to include WIIFM or WIIFC—What's in it for me (the reader) or what's in it for the company.

Many proposal formats exist. Some are even mandated by organizations. If that's the case with your organization or intended audience, follow those guidelines carefully. If you have more flexibility, adapt the following format to match your readers' expectations.

Overview

The Overview, sometimes called an executive summary, contains the most important information for the most readers. It gives the big picture. It will be the only part of the proposal many people read. The overview includes:

Request	What is being proposed?
Business Context	What is the business issue being addressed?
Benefits	How will the proposed solution help the organization (the pros)?
Key Questions	What specific issues are you addressing?
Conclusions	What answers did your investigation reveal?
Recommendations	What actions do you recommend?
Investment	What will it cost and what will be the return on investment?

Discussion

The Discussion explains your reasoning and gives enough evidence to support your conclusions and recommendations. The Discussion covers all of the above in more detail, plus possibly:

Pros and cons
Intended results

Critical success factors
Alternative solutions
Cost breakdown
Process analysis
Implementation schedule
Resource requirements
Vendor analysis
Job plan

Workplace Application—Technical Proposal

The Quality Improvement Proposal in Figure 3-10 illustrates another very simple format. It could be summarized as:

- **Proposal**—Brief summary of technical change requested and benefits to company.

- **Current environment**—What the current practices are.

- **Proposed change**—What actions are required and at what cost.

- **Benefits**—What business results justify the change, especially the financial implications.

Notice that logical organization makes even the most technical information clear. With the main idea up front and sections clearly focused with informative headings, even a lay reader understands the big picture.

To: Internal Client

From: I.M. Analyst

Date: June 7, 200_

Subject: Proposal to Purchase Modems to Reduce Costs

Quality Improvement Proposal

By replacing five 4800 bps modems on monthly rental from BIG PHONE with 56 Kbps modems, we can eliminate lease costs, improve response time, reduce file transfer times (thereby reducing connect-time costs) and better manage the lines required for mainframe dial access by Coal and Petroleum.

Figure 3-10. Quality improvement proposal

Current Environment

- Three lines reserved for dial access by the two mines and the two refineries.

- Two BIG PHONE modems on rent (cost for one modem not found in known BIG PHONE bills) for $294 at Corporate and one each at Mine 1 and Mine 2 for $288.00 per month (total of $582.00).

- One line dedicated for dial-up access at 28 Kbps (ideally should be two) by the Central Region and Mine 1 System/6000 computers as back-up for the X.25 mainframe access to the mainframe.

- A decision has been made to delay installation of the East Kentucky System/6000 until 200_.

Proposed Change

- Purchase three 56K modems (one 14.4K modem has already been purchased by Coal) at a cost of $2,100.00 for Corporate.

- Create a pool of four 56K modems for access by the mines, Central Region, and refineries.

- Have the four sites purchase 56 Kbps modems for a total of $2,800.00 (i.e., 4 modems at $700.00 each). Central Region and Mine 1 have compatible 28 Kbps modems and could retain those if desired.

Benefits/Justification

- Reduce monthly BIG PHONE rentals by $582.00.

- Payout for the modem purchases (a total of $4,900.00) is nine months if the refineries purchase new modems.

- Payout for the modem purchases is six months if the refineries can locate comparable modems already on-hand.

- Decrease on-line response times by nearly two-thirds (e.g., if response time is 6 seconds, a response time of 2-3 seconds can be expected).

- Decrease file transfer time by nearly two-thirds, reducing long distance cost (when connection is primarily for file transfer).

- Improve availability of dial access for the affected locations and potentially reduce total number of lines required.

- Standardization of SDLC dial access at 56 Kbps using the V.32bis modulation standard.

Figure 3-10. Quality improvement proposal *(concluded)*

Practice: Developing a Proposal

Your employer is considering a new performance appraisal policy. In the past, raises were granted based on seniority. The new system would create annual performance reviews, with salary increases tied to those reviews. You have been asked to serve on an employee task force to consider the benefits of such a policy and to propose a plan of action to Mr. Fuller, the manager of Human Resources. Although he is not actively *opposed* to the change, he has been with the organization for years and likes the current seniority system.

In planning, consider such questions as these:

- What are the problems with the current system?

- What are the pros and cons associated with a change?

- What solution(s) do you recommend?

- What benefits does your solution offer?

- What specific actions are necessary to implement a new system (e.g., supervisor-employee meetings, new forms, training)?

- What timetable would you suggest?

Using the space provided, brainstorm ideas to include in your proposal. Then evaluate those ideas and organize them into a working outline for the proposal. Remember to consider your audiences and purpose as you shape your blueprint.

Subject—Proposing New Performance Appraisal Policy

Pros	*Cons*

JUSTIFYING YOUR POINT

In simple proposals, you do not need to analyze pros and cons extensively. You only need to justify the idea you are proposing. In that case, organize details into:

- ■ Your point—what you want to change.

- ■ Your reasons—why the change is beneficial.

- ■ The action requested—what you want your readers to do.

The e-mail in Figure 3-11 exemplifies this model.

Workplace Application—Justifying a Change

From: Sam Manager
To: Ed Supervisor
Date: Mon., June 21, 200_
Subject: NEW REPORTING HOURS

Eddie,

Let's consider changing our hours to 6:00 a.m. until 2:30 p.m. This will enable us to accomplish several things. Of course, beating some of the afternoon heat is the main consideration, but it will also help to avoid a lot of the morning traffic by having the crews out of the yard no later than 6:30. I think too that we will see less conflict between the public and the trim crews, especially around park spray pools and shelters. Give this some consideration, and let me know what you decide. We will need a letter informing the employees affected.

Figure 3-11. Justifying your point

Would this e-mail be even clearer if broken into three paragraphs? If so, where would you divide it?

Practice: Write an e-mail to your supervisor requesting a change in office procedure or permission to purchase a piece of equipment.

CONVEYING 5 Ws AND H INFORMATION

Sometimes your sole purpose is to convey information about something: announcing a decision, setting a meeting, reporting on a trip. In that case, brainstorm your ideas with the 5 Ws and H of the newspaper reporter: Who, What, When, Where, Why, and How. Frequently these are organized into the model in Figure 3-12.

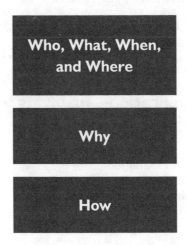

Figure 3-12. 5 Ws and H information

Workplace Application—Informational Memo

The informational memo in Figure 3-13 shows a good meeting announcement. Identify the 5 Ws and H. Which one is missing? How will readers use this document?

To: D.P. Department
From: Sue Smith
Date: January 3, 200_
Subject: Online Statements

On Wednesday, January 13, 200_, we will be meeting in the D.P. Conference Room to discuss Online Statements. This meeting will take 30 minutes so that we may cover the following topics:

Scope of the Project
    Do we need online statements for DDA, Savings, CDs, and ILD?
    What type of hardcopy facilities will be needed?

Constraints
    What is our time frame?

Structure
    What information is to be displayed and how will it be formatted?

Figure 3-13. Informational memo

USING A PROBLEM-SOLVING STRATEGY

While your purpose sometimes is strictly to convey information, most business writing is persuasive. Using a problem-solving strategy sells the readers your idea clearly and effectively. In fact, most workplace documents—reports, proposals, letters, memos, and e-mail—are written to solve problems.

The complexity of your writing task determines the specific information in each section. For example, in the report format the Overview covers the problem (business context) and solution (conclusions and recommendations). For very short memos, e-mails, and letters, you may need only a few paragraphs (see Figure 3-14).

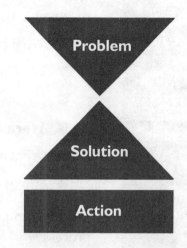

Figure 3-14. Problem/solution model

Workplace Application—Problem-Solving Memo

The memo in Figure 3-15 reveals a clear problem-solution strategy.

Date: April 23, 200_

To: Mildred Coworker

From: Teresa R. Banker

Subject: Notification of Deposit Receipt

Thank you for bringing the problem concerning interoffice mailing of your notification of deposit to our attention. Please let me assure you that I share your concern for the confidentiality of <u>all</u> bank customers, including our own personnel.

In the future, all correspondence for bank personnel concerning Certificate of Deposits and Savings accounts will be sealed in standard windowed envelopes and routed through the mail room.

Please accept my apology for the indiscretion.

Figure 3-15. Problem-solving memo

Organizing

An experienced consultant tells about reviewing a three-page procedure written for a municipal water plant. The first sentence said, "Flip Switch A." Three pages later, at the end of the procedure, came this warning: "Note: You must work quickly. When you flip Switch A, you turn off power to the plant."

What's wrong with this picture?

EXPLAINING A PROCEDURE

When you explain how to do something, always assume that you have inexperienced readers. Why would someone read a procedure carefully if he or she already knew what to do? That means a good procedure will orient the readers *up front* about six possible Ws:

- **What** the procedure achieves or why it is important.

- **Who** is responsible for the procedure?

- If it involves a change, **why** the change was made.

- **When** it applies.

- **What** equipment, materials, and manuals to gather.

- Any **warnings** or special notes.

The traditional procedure resembles a story: Here is how this process works. However, modern procedures look more like a script: Who is the actor and what are the actions? The step-by-step explanation uses the Actor/Act details you brainstormed in planning if more than one person is involved. Identify the actors and action steps in chronological order, renaming each actor when responsibility shifts.

Both experienced readers and novices need clear headings to help them find the particular information they seek. The steps themselves should be action-oriented. Of course, the procedure must be complete.

The procedure in Figure 3-16 is reader-friendly because it clearly tells readers what to expect, including potential problems and the correct results. It then lays out what to do and what will result from each action—a variation on Actor/Act. Another good example of a claims filing procedure, with clearly sequenced action steps, appears in Chapter 4, "Writing."

During a patient's two-week follow-up appointment with his cardiologist, he informed his doctor that he was having trouble with one of his medications. "Which one?" the doctor asked. "The patch. The nurse told me to put on a new one every six hours, and now I'm running out of places to put it!" The doctor had him quickly undress and discovered what she hoped she wouldn't see. . . . Yes, the man had over 50 patches on his body! Now the instructions include removal of the old patch before applying a new one.

Using the LAN

Introduction
Because of the way the LAN is attached to the mainframe, you may experience some mainframe problems:

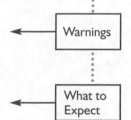

- Documents may not print correctly.

- You may get stuck with the X( ) for a long period of time.

Printing documents
Always print your documents from the View the Document screen. If you print from the Work with the Document screen, you will print the unformatted version of the document.

Even if you print correctly, the document will not print exactly like it did before you were attached to the LAN. These things will be different:

- An extra line will be printed at the top of each document indicating what version of SCRIPT/VS is being used.

- The document will print very close to the left edge of the paper.

How to restart when you get stuck on the X( ).

	Action	Result
1	From the menu bar of your mainframe session, point to **Session** and click	Drop down menu displays
2	Point to **Power off** and click	Window becomes blank
3	Point to **Session** and click	Drop down menu displays
4	Point to **Close Session** and click	[Not Connected] message displays on the title bar
5	Point to **Session** and click	Drop down menu displays
6	Point to **Open Session** and click	Open Session dialog box displays
7	Select the session you want to open and click on [OK]	Mainframe menu appears

Figure 3-16. Reader-friendly procedure

WRITING ACTION-ORIENTED PROCEDURES

Passive verbs in the traditional procedure style pose a major danger of ambiguity. The lack of an "actor" makes unclear who is responsible for doing the action. (See Chapter 5, "Editing," for a more thorough discussion of passive verbs.)

Instead of Passive: "The following changes **need to be made**."
                                                                passive

                        By whom?

Try Active: "Please **make** the following changes."
                                            active

Passives add unnecessary words, create a low-impact voice, and mask responsibility; the active style is concise, energetic, and clear.

Workplace Application— Action-Oriented Procedures

The original and revised procedure/request in Figure 3-17 and Figure 3-18 illustrates how clarity increased when the writer chose an active style.

To: Robert Peters
From: Betty Dean
Date: October 18, 200_
Re: Change to Percent Current Production Reports

As you may remember from the meeting we had with K. C. Smith, some changes need to be made to this report.

For Coal only, a separate report should be created for customers "00011", "00022", and "00033"; and these customers excluded from the primary report. The new report should be titled "Percent Current—Voluntary Pay Customers".

For all segments, the negative balances being excluded from the main reports should now be included and the separate totalling for them in the "unadjusted totals" should be eliminated. All segments will need a month-end version to be run on the 7th or 8th work nights. This version will need to incorporate any items on the closed item file which were still open on the last day of the month.

I don't know if Treasury still wants the Friday night version currently in production—check out with K.C. Smith or David Case.

Figure 3-17. Original procedure

To: Robert Peters

From: Betty Dean

Date: October 18, 200_

Re: **Change to Percent Current Production Reports**

As we discussed in our meeting with K.C. Smith, please make the following changes to the Percent Current reports:

- For Coal only, create a separate report for customers "00011", "00022", and "00033". Title the new report "Percent Current—Voluntary Pay Customers." Then exclude those customers from the primary report.

- For all segments, change the reports so that they no longer exclude negative balances. When you make this change, you will not need that coding which creates the "unadjusted totals." Take it out.

- Set up a month-end version of the report to run on the seventh or eighth work night. Add any invoices to this report from the closed item file which were still open on the last day of the month. Create an extract file similar to the one you did for the month-end aging reports to add to these items.

Once you've made these changes, it would probably be a good idea to ask K.C. Smith and David Case if they still want Friday night production runs for these reports. My guess is they will not.

cc: Barbara Fowler
    Dale Jones
    K.C. Smith
    David Case
    Jason Mason

Figure 3-18. Revised procedure

MODERNIZING YOUR LETTERS

Letters, by tradition, are the most formal type of document because they go to outsiders—customers, regulators, vendors, and business associates. Unfortunately, the formal tradition has often frozen both the format and the style of letters in the nineteenth century. Changes in the modern workplace—in technology (computers, fax) and in audience (unknown addressees and gender)—now dictate a more contemporary style. The letter in Figure 3-19 is outdated in format and style—and not very clear.

Workplace Application—Outdated vs. Modern Style

```
                                          March 3, 200_


County Courthouse
500 South Denver
City, State 94103


Attention:  County Assessor

Gentlemen:

Please provide me with the information of whether or not
you assess ad valorem taxes on the following types of
properties in your county:

    Mineral Producing         _____

    Mineral Non-Producing _____

Please return this information in the enclosed self-
addressed, postage-paid envelope.

                                     Sincerely,

                                     George W. Smith

                                     George W. Smith
                                     Tax Department



GWS/bg
Enclosure
```

Figure 3-19. Outdated letter style

March 3, 200_

County Courthouse
500 South Denver
City, ST 94103

Attention: County Assessor

Do you assess ad valorem taxes on the following types of properties in your county?

Mineral Producing _____

Non-Mineral Producing _____

Please return this information in the enclosed envelope, or fax it to 909-555-4321. Thank you for your help.

George W. Smith

George W. Smith
Tax Department

GWS/bg
enclosure

Figure 3-20. Modern letter style

Is the simplified version of the same letter in Figure 3-20 appropriate and clear? If so, why? What has changed?

In modern letter style, you may:

■ Use full block paragraphs and page layout (no indentations) for a more readable format. In addition, studies show that a left-justified and ragged right margin is more readable than a fully justified margin. Spreading the letters to fully justify text reduces readability.

■ Replace the salutation with an attention line, especially if the letter serves the same purpose as an office-to-office memo or if you do not know the gender of the addressee.

■ Omit the complimentary close if you omit the salutation.

■ Omit courtesy titles (Mr., Mrs., and Ms.) in the address lines, except for formal occasions. If you use a title, Ms. is generally accepted for females, but follow the addressee's preference. Indicate professional titles either by placing the degree abbreviation after the name or by using Dr. before the name.

◼ Use a comma instead of a colon in a personal business letter salutation.

◼ Ask direct questions.

◼ Use headings and bulleted lists to make text more readable.

◼ Use "you," "I," and "we." Personal pronouns give letters a warm, human voice.

Chapter 5, "Editing," includes additional strategies for achieving a direct, personal style and contains additional sample letters.

Practice: Responding to an Angry Former Customer

The customer service group of a regional bank's credit card division received the letter in Figure 3-21 from George Hotunderthecollar.

Gentlemen:

Enclosed please find my check for 48.86 which will pay my bill in full less the following deductions.

Interested Charge	7.48
	12.00
	19.40

Since you were so nice to cancel my card for no reason or at least you could of issue me another under another number without the statement your card has been cancelled. I feel I am entitled to at least 3/4 of my fee I paid you for the use of your card for a year. In addition to that I feel you took the auto club for a ride just to increase your card business. Dirty Pool I Call it. Furthermore I considered it a reflection on my credit when you cancelled my card. You have always been paid in full way ahead of the due date except this last time which was a slip in my bookkeeping. My credit is more important to me than anything else. In fact that is why my wife and I got a devorce but it was not over a charge accont but a lot bigger sum on a business.

I am still considering haveing a class mate which is a lawyer file a suit against you. I may not win but it dam sure cost you some money. I am expecting a letter from you.

Sincerly,
George Hotunderthecollar

Figure 3-21. Angry customer letter

Organizing

Mr. Hotunderthecollar was correct. He did have a good credit rating and did not deserve to have his card cancelled, based on his payment record.

However, the bank had to cancel his card because of the divorce. The original account was for both parties, and bank policy required canceling any jointly held accounts. In addition, the card had been issued through an agreement with the auto club, a contract that was expiring. The auto club prohibited the bank from soliciting new accounts from former cardholders, so the bank could not offer to open a new account under the gentleman's own name.

Unfortunately, when Mr. Hotunderthecollar wrote to drop his ex-wife's name from the account, no one explained the situation to him. He simply received a cancellation notice plus interest due.

Mr. Hotunderthecollar is "expecting a letter." In responding, brainstorm details you might want to include, organize your points, and then write a draft. Be sure to arrange points based on what is important to Mr. Hotunderthecollar.

PREWRITING WORKSPACE

COMMUNICATING ELECTRONICALLY

E-mail is replacing memos and letters. Traditionally, a letter was a formal communication with external audiences; memos were less formal because they reached internal audiences. New technology has destroyed those distinctions. E-mail and fax—new *delivery* methods—routinely zap messages to both internal and external readers.

Despite this pervasive usage, e-mail is *perceived* to be an extremely informal medium, almost like a personal conversation, which may lack clear organization, verbal precision, or grammatical care. For personal e-mail between friends, such a conversational tone may be okay. But for a business e-mail, the result can be a decidedly reader-unfriendly—and unprofessional—message.

Consider the advantages and disadvantages of e-mail shown in Table 3-1.

Table 3-1. Advantages and Disadvantages of E-mail

Advantages	Disadvantages
• Convenient, quick • Get instant answers • Can easily send multiple copies • References are attached • Can access any time and place • Saves paper • Low cost • Documented (written, permanent) • Encourages teamwork • Gives you time to cool off	• "Dirty"—grammar errors and rambling • Delayed (or unknown) responses • Junk mail • Scavenger hunts or bad "chain letters" • NOT private • Have a life of their own • Legally binding • Hard to erase • Hard to find for later reference • Lose tone of voice and personality
Ferris Research estimates the overall benefit of e-mail "in terms of increased productivity equals about $9,000 per employee." —Dan Dieterich Communication Consultant	"It's as ubiquitous as winter damp, a pernicious miasma that brings rot and ruin to society's delicate underpinnings. I speak of e-mail, the greatest threat to civilization since lead dinnerware addled the brains of the Roman aristocracy." —Seth Shostak <u>Newsweek</u>
"E-mail is a stack of dynamite with your name on it." —Unknown	

Maximizing E-mail

To improve your electronic communication, follow these guidelines:

Manage the medium.

■ *Choose your medium wisely.* Is it better to call or write? Is e-mail, which is an impersonal medium, the best way to achieve the result you want? Should you call instead, for example, regarding personnel matters, changing an agreement, or establishing a time frame? Or should you write a letter or memorandum?

■ *Send less.* Everyone is buried in information these days. Send only messages that count (e.g., do not thank someone for thanking you!).

■ *Target your distribution list.* People stop reading when they receive too many messages. Include only those readers who need your message. "Fan-out messages" waste everyone's time.

■ *Establish organizational guidelines.* Determine as an organization what type of messages are appropriate. Do you want employees to use e-mail for personal business, telling jokes, advertising their garage sales, or selling charity raffle tickets? Violating e-mail policy may be grounds for termination.

Treat e-mail as a "real" document.

■ *Use principles of good writing.* Plan, organize, edit, and refine. Focus on meeting your audiences' needs for information, style, and clarity.

■ *Think before you write.* E-mail is **not** a conversation. You should treat it like any written document by planning and organizing before you write. Remember: E-mail has all the legal standing of any written document. Plus, it goes farther, faster, to more people. As Col. Oliver North testified during the Iran Contra investigation, "We all sincerely believed that when we sent a PROFS [e-mail] message to another party and punched the button 'delete' that it was gone forever. Boy, were we wrong."

Organizing

■ *Get to the point.* The first paragraph should tell your readers the point you are making. E-mail can become a bad chain letter or scavenger hunt. You have to read from bottom to top to figure out the main idea. Also, your subject line should cover the point. Readers may not open the document if the subject line is not clearly focused.

■ *Be diplomatic.* Because e-mail seems like a conversation, we can respond too quickly. We sometimes write things that tone of voice or humor would soften, but on the cold, hard screen sound inappropriate or rude. Cool off before you respond and then have damage to control.

An overburdened worker actually answered multiple requests about a new database by writing, "At the risk of opening up a can of worms that I defiantly [*sic*] do not have the time to respond to, I wanted to try to give some information to you. . . . If you are just curious because you think I have some new fangled tracking system or whatever, I have a number of responsibilities that come first. Please E-MAIL your request. Please do not call me, e-mail me, inter-company me the same day, the very next day, etc. . . . Okay, I guess that's it and I'll stand by for the worms to start crawling out of that can now."

■ *Follow standard capitalization rules.* Typing in all capitals is perceived as shouting; all lower case is poetic but improper. Both are hard to read and invite more punctuation errors.

■ *Proofread.* E-mail should be quick but not dirty. If you overlook spelling and punctuation errors, if you don't care about sentence structure, your readers have to translate. Reader-friendly writing—even electronically—requires the courtesy of quality control.

> "All messages going outside the organization—regardless of whether the messages are in paper or e-mail form—should therefore be treated as if they were official organization records and conform to a specified writing standard—addressing content, type of language, use of slang, grammar and spelling requirements, review, etc. This writing standard would also be appropriate for all official records only maintained internally."
>
> —Donald S. Skupsky

Practice: Focusing E-mail

The e-mail in Figure 3-22 is complete but indirect. Without a clear main idea and strong key points, readers will have to figure out the writer's point. Reorganize the e-mail using one of the organizational models discussed in this chapter: proposal, point/reasons, or problem/solution/action. Then rewrite the e-mail. Remember to focus the subject line.

To:	George Johnson
From:	Sam Simpson
Cc:	Robert Martin, David Whitman, Matt Jones, George James
Subject:	Carlin Conduits

George, I spoke with Matt and Gary Winston today. Gary said the electrical contractor suggested that when the building is moved, they leave all those conduits there and make a large junction box there and reuse some of those old conduits.

I would like to express my opinion on this matter, if you are considering this change. When I first looked at this project I thought that would be what we could do but, after giving some thought to it, I remembered all those conduits out there surrounding the building! There are TONS of conduits around that building! Some of these conduits are hard to identify. There have been so many conduits installed over the years so close to each other and running every which way, that reusing these will compound the problem. I think it would be advantageous to tear out many of those and run new, in a logical uncrowded manner. In the future, there will be no question a) which conduit b) exactly how it's routed c) where it is d) if Gary is the inspector, he will know within inches where someone can dig or set something. e) New wire will be multi-conductor cable whereas, most of those old conduits contain single conductor and could be too small.

The difference in price will be worth it with ease of identity and orderly routing.

Can you tell which way I'm leaning?
Thanks,
Sam

Figure 3-22. Indirect message

Organizing

PREWRITING _WORKSPACE_

DESIGNING YOUR DOCUMENT

New technology allows us to produce more readable documents, *if* we think beyond our traditional concepts of what text looks like. It is still important to organize ideas and details logically in a well-focused blueprint. Then we can add an architecture, making the shape of the document clear. Studies show that headings, white space with lists, and even side-by-side text can make documents far more reader-friendly. Unfortunately, many writers still produce text as if it came from Gutenberg's fifteenth-century press—dense paragraphs and no visual appeal.

This book contains multiple examples of modern document design. Revisit the following examples to see how their designs move beyond logical organization to improve clarity:

- Revised e-mail in Figure 3-4
- Easy response form in Figure 3-6
- Internal audit report format in Figure 3-8
- Technical proposal in Figure 3-10
- Reader-friendly procedure in Figure 3-16

In addition, the book itself uses lists, columns, diagrams, and sidebars throughout—all elements designed to make your job as reader easier.

Workplace Application—Document Design

The original and redesigned memos in Figure 3-23 and Figure 3-24 illustrate the importance of document design. The original memo, developed to control high turnover and improve employee reliability, was complete and logically organized. Employees received it as part of their new employee orientation. However, notice how much more reader-friendly the redesigned version is.

Analyze the original and redesigned versions by answering these questions:

- How do you think employees responded to the original?
- What are the key points it makes?
- What did the writer change to improve readability in the redesigned version?
- What stands out?
- How could employees use the redesigned version?

Organizing

Maintenance Division

TO: New Maintenance Employee

FROM: Sam Smithson
                 Superintendent

SUBJECT: Expectations and Responsibilities

As the successful applicant for this position, we welcome you to the Maintenance Division!

There are some very important expectations and responsibilities associated with this position that we want to share with you. Your overall attendance (sick leave, AWOL's, tardies, LWOP's) needs to be maintained at an acceptable level as required in the Division policies. Good attendance is critical because the Maintenance Division is responsible for emergency services to citizens in the City. The entire section must respond to these calls as quickly as possible, and your absence may affect getting the job completed quickly and efficiently. Failure to maintain good attendance during your probationary period will result in your immediate termination.

In order to successfully complete the six-month probationary period and maintain your position in this Division, you must have good attendance and be performing all of your job duties at a satisfactory level by the end of the six months probation. Service Writer, Master Mechanics, Mechanics, and Mechanic Helpers must also obtain a Class "A" Commercial Driver's License.

It is extremely important that you follow supervisory instructions and display a cooperative, positive attitude at all times while conducting City business, including in your offices, in training sessions or any portion of the office complex. You will be expected to conduct yourself in a professional manner when interacting with other employees, your supervisors, citizens and vendors—treating everyone with dignity and respect.

You must perform your job, not only effectively and efficiently, but **safely**. Following safe working procedures is a **job requirement**. A high percentage of accidents and job injuries are a result of employees violating common safety practices and procedures. Accidents and/or injuries could be reduced or eliminated by employees simply understanding the importance of practicing safety both on and off the job. Because accidents and injuries add substantially to the cost of delivering services to our citizens, they must be kept to a minimum.

Congratulations on your new position in our organization, and we are confident you will enjoy a successful career in the Maintenance Division.

_____   Date_____

Employee Signature

_____   Date_____

Witness Signature

Figure 3-23. Original memo

Maintenance Division

To: New Maintenance Employee

From: Sam Smithson, Superintendent

Subject: Expectations and Responsibilities

Welcome to Maintenance! Some very important responsibilities are associated with your position.

Probationary Requirements

To successfully complete the six-month probationary period and keep your position in this Division, you must:

- Maintain your overall attendance (sick leave, AWOLs, LWOPs, tardies) at the satisfactory level defined in the Division policies. During your probation, unsatisfactory attendance will result in immediate termination.
- Perform all job duties at a satisfactory level by the end of the six months.
- Service Writer, Master Mechanics, Mechanics, and Mechanic Helpers **must** also acquire and maintain a Class "A" Commercial Driver's License.

Personal Conduct

You must follow supervisory instructions and display a cooperative, positive attitude while conducting City business, including in City offices and vehicles, in training sessions, or in any portion of the office complex. When interacting with other employees, your supervisors, citizens and vendors, conduct yourself in a professional manner—treating everyone with dignity and respect.

Safety

Violating safety practices and procedures causes accidents and job injuries which add substantially to the cost of delivering services to our citizens. By following City and Division safety policies, you can perform your job effectively, efficiently, and **safely**.

Congratulations on your new position in our organization, and we are confident you will enjoy a successful career in the Maintenance Division.

_____   Date_____
Employee Signature

_____   Date_____
Witness Signature

Figure 3-24. Redesigned memo

Graphics Tips for Creating Readable Documents

Good document design follows the KIS principle—Keep It Simple! Follow these guidelines in using the design elements that new technology provides:

Fonts

■ Use serif fonts like Times New Roman, Garamond, or Palatino Linotype for continuous text. According to studies, the horizontal elements at the base of the letters carry the reader's eyes forward, linking the words.

■ Use sans serif fonts like Arial, Tahoma, or Verdana for headings. The unfooted style emphasizes a free-standing element.

■ Limit the number of font types on a page to three.

■ Avoid casual fonts like Comic Sans or *Monotype Corsiva* in professional documents.

■ Prefer moderately weighted fonts like Times New Roman. A thick font like **Impact** or a thin font like MS Mincho are hard to read.

■ Choose a font size from 10 to 12 points for text and larger for headings.

Emphasis

■ Emphasize words by using **bold**, *italics*, or color.

■ Avoid underlining and ALL CAPS, which interfere with reading.

Layout

■ Use full block style, with all text elements left-justified and no paragraph indentation.

■ Choose symbols to mark lists that are appropriate to their content.

■ Use numbered lists if you are enumerating or presenting a chronological sequence.

■ Use bulleted lists to indicate like items or ideas, usually in descending order of importance.

■ Make lists parallel in structure—that is, all phrases, all action statements, or all sentences.

■ Avoid inappropriate background templates—for example, in e-mail. They are unprofessional looking and take longer to download.

Writing

Potential Problems	Strategies
Paragraph covers more than one topic.	Write strong, controlling topic sentences. Limit each paragraph to one key point and supporting details.
Paragraph is not arranged logically.	Plan paragraphs before you write by: ■ Jotting down the details; ■ Arranging points in logical order and adding transitions; ■ Placing your topic sentence at the beginning of the paragraph.
Paragraph requires too much concentration to follow.	Use visual clues such as headings and lists.
Relationship of one paragraph to the next is not clear.	Connect paragraphs with standard transitions and paragraph hooks.
Document is text-heavy.	Use graphics if they convey details more clearly than words do.

CHAPTER 4—WRITING

WRITING THE DOCUMENT

Have you ever struggled through a document, feeling lost and frustrated, working hard at understanding by reading and then rereading? Who's doing the work there? Wandering paragraphs, buried points, lack of logical direction, dense text—these symptoms of poor organization mean the writer expects the reader to create meaning out of raw information.

But it's the writer's job to do the thinking. Having organized your ideas into a high-level map, you focus on writing the draft—filling in your general design with details. Some experts encourage students to freewrite to discover their ideas while they create text. That approach works if you need a topic for an essay, but in the workplace you generally know your topic. Brainstorming first, then writing from a well-designed map is usually more efficient than writing to discover.

This chapter completes the answer to "What Are My Key Points?"—the logical development of key points in paragraphs. Even though this is a very basic subject, poorly focused paragraphs can be a serious problem. Without organization, key points are buried or omitted. Then interested readers must search for points and may misinterpret data; disinterested readers stop reading. Writing clear paragraphs allows your readers to find information efficiently.

Well-written paragraphs depend on:

- Understanding the relationship of specific details to more abstract concepts;

- Developing strong topic sentences that clarify key points;

- Focusing on one key point per paragraph;

- Creating a logical flow so that readers stay on track;

- Integrating text and visuals when a graphic will be more reader-friendly.

THE LADDER OF ABSTRACTION

The English language contains a wide spectrum of terms for any given thing, ranging from very concrete, specific, visual terms like "cow" through gradually more general and abstract terms like "livestock," "farm assets," and "resources." The Ladder of Abstraction, a concept popularized by S. I. Hayakawa in *Language in Thought and Action*, helps us understand both how language works and how to use it to write well. This ladder shows that effective communication depends on clearly relating words to the things, people, or ideas they represent.

The example of the word "profit" in Figure 4-1 follows the progression from the object itself to concrete/specific terms to abstract words, moving from the bottom *up* the ladder.

The process of abstracting, a crucial human ability to think and speak in more general terms, involves noting similarities and ignoring differences. Humans need to communicate in general terms, to be able to group ideas or products or persons. We could not analyze "profits" or "programs" or "personnel" without the ability to abstract.

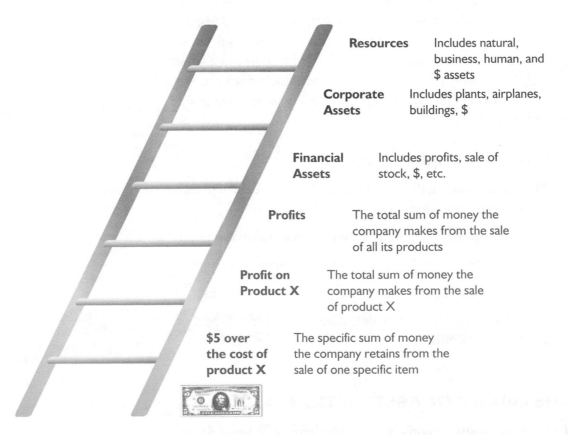

Figure 4-1. The Ladder of Abstraction. Adapted from S. I. Hayakawa, *Language in Thought and Action*, 4th edition (Boston: Heinle, 1978). Copyright 1978 by Heinle, a division of Thomson Learning. Reprinted with permission.

Using the Ladder to Organize

However, the Ladder of Abstraction reveals the tendency of some writers and speakers to get stuck at one level. This dead-level abstracting sometimes occurs at a low level: A writer who presents only data without ever generalizing or drawing conclusions leaves readers wondering, "What is the point?" Dead level abstracting also occurs at a high level, in the clouds of abstract thinking. "Theories," "strategies," "planning," "vision," and "goals" are meaningful words only when tied to the specifics they represent.

Thus, the issue is not whether we should use abstractions. We must. The issue, instead, concerns *how* we use abstractions. Effective writing moves freely up and down the ladder, presenting abstract statements as the main idea and key points and then supporting them with specific evidence, examples, and explanation.

Using the Ladder to Edit

The Ladder of Abstraction also gives insights into developing a clear style. Good writers choose specific or concrete words as low on the ladder as possible. For example,

- "A profit of $5 per widget" is more precise than "a good profit."

- "A bus that seats 32 people" is clearer than "adequate transportation."

- "Please respond before March 1" is more accurate than "Please respond at your earliest convenience."

The Ladder of Abstraction reminds you to decide, "How much detail should I include so that my readers understand?" and "What words should I choose to be clear?"

WRITING PARAGRAPHS

A paragraph is a group of sentences that fully explain one idea so that your readers clearly understand both your reasoning and the evidence that supports that reasoning. To accomplish this purpose, a fully developed paragraph has two parts:

1. A strong topic sentence that states your general key point

2. Logically arranged details, or specific evidence, that fully explain the key point

Deciding How Long a Paragraph Should Be

There is no rule governing paragraph length. To completely explain a key point, a standard paragraph usually contains between 50 and 150 words. However, paragraphs in short letters, memos, and e-mail with very limited topics may be shorter. But very short paragraphs (one or two sentences each) suggest that the key point has not been fully explained; with scanty evidence, the reader may not be convinced. On the other hand, a paragraph that is too long may not clearly focus on just one topic. You should consider dividing paragraphs that are too long or unfocused to give each key point the attention it deserves and sometimes simply to give the reader's eye a rest.

> One wag suggested, "A paragraph should be like a woman's skirt: long enough to cover the topic, but short enough to be interesting."

Focusing Key Points in Topic Sentences

A strong topic sentence is the key to effective paragraphing. It tells the reader what to expect in the rest of the paragraph. However, it is not enough to say, "The next topic is the use of computers in the workplace." A good topic sentence names both the *topic* and your *point* about that topic; it focuses and directs the paragraph. Therefore, each topic sentence should identify both your topic and your point (or controlling idea) about that topic.

For example:

> *Topic (T)*   *Point (P)*
> **Computers** are now **essential** to American industry.

Readers expect to find the topic sentence at the beginning of the paragraph. We tend to think inductively: Gather data and then draw a conclusion or point. If we write that way, the topic sentence shows up at the end of the paragraph. But readers generally do not want to think with the writer. They prefer a deductive, point-first structure.

Workplace Application— Good Topic Sentences

Notice how these topic sentences clearly direct the following two paragraphs.

Business Example

> P   T
>
> The team has determined that **no further reduction** of **paperwork** is possible at the present growth rate (see attached report). Other actions anticipated to further reduce the amount of paperwork are being investigated by other teams; therefore, the Quality Council recommended that this team be closed. Susan will continue to monitor copier usage for the next few months to evaluate the cause of any trends that may occur. Changes will be reported to Miguel Ordonez for action as necessary.

Technical Example

> T   P
>
> The **installation** of Shadowing is rather **painless**. It requires loading the software onto the system, running Systeware's installation programs, and doing an update to the system from an SLT tape created during the installation process. The one drawback is that it has to be performed with no one accessing the system. You also have the support and backing of the support personnel 24 hours a day in the event that problems do occur with the installation. I have already installed a demo copy of this software on the system and had no problems doing the installation.

Practice: Topic Sentences

T   P

Underline and label the **topic** and **point** words in these sentences :

1. In the meeting, we will set guidelines for making our group more efficient.

2. The new vacation schedule is more practical than the old one.

3. The last project illustrates the problems created by the meddling of EMA investigators.

4. The tasks of this position can be grouped into three categories: administrative, clerical, and bookkeeping.

5. We must choose between two types of laboratory equipment.

Readers usually are more interested in what you *learned* than in what you did. The following paragraphs are narratives of what happened. Storytelling is appropriate for some paragraphs, such as a background section. However, focusing on a sequence of events can bury or omit the key point.

Writing

Practice: Buried Topic Sentences

Move the buried topic sentence or create a topic sentence for each of the following paragraphs. Your goal is to put the *key point* up front.

1. On February 1, 1994, I performed air monitoring tests in the engine room at the Fareview station. The reason for the air monitoring was to identify any presence of an organic vapor. I used a device called PHOAC—Photo Detector Model. It measures organic vapor in ppm, parts per million. I took sixteen separate readings in various areas in the engine, with the concentration on the Allo units. At the time of the testing, both units were operating. If there were a time when any organic vapors would be released, it should be when the units are operating. (Attached is a plot plan of the performed testing.) The results of the testing showed **absolutely no readings** of organic vapors in the engine room.

2. A tally of telephone calls inquiring into job openings was kept over a 1-month time period. It is estimated that approximately 1 to 1½ hours per day is spent on the telephone in response to these inquiries. The "job line" would allow Personnel employees to concentrate more of their time and efforts in other areas of the employment process. Southwest Energy, General Maintenance, and Advanced Equipment Company are a few of the major employers who utilize a job line to list job openings.

3. Currently deal sheets are filled out by hand by the traders and then given to the contract administrator. The contract administrator enters the data into a database and then deal reports are generated and given to the other users of the information who re-enter the information for their applications. The same information gets keyed five or six times.

CREATING PARAGRAPH UNITY

A strong topic sentence forces you to stick to the topic by clearly focusing on the key point. This focus is called **paragraph unity**. That means that all elements of the paragraph work together to explain one idea. An effective paragraph includes all relevant information, but leaves out unrelated details, no matter how interesting they may be.

Workplace Application—Paragraph Focus

How does this paragraph wander from the key point?

> The filing method in which five trays were removed appeared to be inefficient and counter-productive. In an effort to substantiate or refute the employee's claim, two samples were taken during the productivity survey. Again, during the first week, trays were left in the machines, while during the second week trays were removed.

Workplace Application—Choppy Paragraphs

You should also avoid a series of one sentence paragraphs, such as those in the following letter. Which sentences could be combined in paragraphs?

> Dear Engineer:
>
> This letter is in reference to your request for a copy of the atlas.
>
> Your request has been approved by Supervisor and has been forwarded to Reproduction. A copy of the atlas will be delivered to your location within two weeks.
>
> Your office will be added to our distribution list and updates will be sent to you accordingly.
>
> If you have any questions, please call me at extension ____.
>
> Sincerely,
>
> Chief Draftsman

Writing

WORKSPACE

Imagine that you've been asked to pick up some important information in Bug Tussle this afternoon. You agree, but then discover there's no map to Bug Tussle and they've taken down all the road signs. You do know to head north.

You probably face a long afternoon—getting lost, stopping for directions, taking wrong turns, growing more and more frustrated. At best, the trip takes longer than it should. At worst, you give up and head home.

Your readers face the same frustration if you send them on an "information journey" without a good map and clear road signs along the way. Lost in detail, they may decide not to read at all. If they do finish the journey, you've wasted their time.

Drawing a complete map with good transitions is critical. You can't tell someone how to find Bug Tussle until you know where it is yourself.

MAKING PARAGRAPHS FLOW

Effective paragraphs are also coherent, or orderly, so that one sentence flows logically into the next. You create this flow in four ways:

1. Arrange details in **logical order**.

2. Add clear **transitions** from one sentence to the next.

3. Include **echo words**, or repetitions of certain important words to reinforce the key point.

4. Create a **logical chain** of sentences by moving the reader from old knowledge (known) to new information.

Logical Order

Common sense usually determines the arrangement of details. The following are common patterns:

1. From *general to specific*: for example, applying a point of law to a specific case.

2. From *specific to general*: for example, presenting scientific data before drawing the conclusion. This arrangement can put your topic sentence at the end of the paragraph.

3. In *chronological order*: for example, describing a method of investigation or a history of events.

4. In *visual order*: for example, describing some machinery.

5. From *least important to most important*: for example, identifying or explaining reasons to justify a decision. This traditional approach assumes that readers will remember the last point best *and* that they read the entire paragraph or document.

6. From *most important to least important*: for example, outlining the reasons to accept a proposal or to buy a product. Most workplace readers prefer this order because it focuses on their key concerns first.

As a general rule, the first and last positions—whether in a sentence, a paragraph, or a document—are the strongest and most remembered.

Writing

Transitions

To help your reader follow your logical direction, you must supply the road signs, or transitions from one sentence to the next. Transitional words and phrases show how the details in the paragraph relate. Some frequently used transitions include:

Addition: Also, too, again, in addition, next, finally, last

Comparison: Similarly, likewise, like, bulleted lists (•, •, •)

Contrast: But, yet, however, still, on the other hand, on the contrary, otherwise

Enumeration: First, second, third, 1, 2, 3,…

Illustration: That is, i.e., for example, e.g., for instance

Place: Here, there, beyond, nearby, on the opposite side

Result: Therefore, thus, hence, as a result, consequently

Summary: In other words, in fact, in summary, in short

Time: Immediately, then, soon, often, later, afterward

In addition, **personal pronouns**, such as "he," "she," "it," "they," and demonstrative pronouns, such as "this," "these," and "that," are also transitions of a sort. They point backward to the noun they replace, linking the two in a continuous thought.

Workplace Application— Claims Filing Procedure

Analyze the logical order and the clear transitions of the procedure for filing medical claims in Figure 4-2.

CLAIMS FILING PROCEDURE

Please read these instructions carefully before you present a claim. Effective use on your part of the information given below will assure prompt processing of your claim. Your claim must be received by the Plan Administrator within 24 months from the date on which the expense was incurred. Failure to meet this deadline will prevent your claim from being reimbursed under the Plan.

Preparation of Your Bills

In preparing your bills, the following points should be considered:

First   Become familiar with eligible and ineligible expenses listed in this handbook.

Second   Submit only the unaltered original (<u>not</u> a copy) of each bill. All bills must be itemized. Each bill should show:

a.   the name of the patient and the name and employee number of Employee;
b.   the nature of the illness or injury;
c.   the type of service or supply furnished;
d.   the date, or dates, that the service was rendered or the purchase was made;
e.   the charge for each service or supply;
f.   prescription drug bills will be handled under the provisions of the Prescription Drug Program (see p.1).

Cancelled checks, cash register "receipts" and bills showing only a "balance forward" are not acceptable. All bills must be legible.

Third   Where convenient, bills should be accumulated until (1) treatment has been concluded and your claim is complete, or (2) treatment is continuing and the accumulated expenses represent a significant sum, at least equal to the deductible amount, if any.

Remember, claims submitted later than 24 months after the date the charges were incurred are ineligible.

Figure 4-2. Claims filing procedure

Writing

Echo Words

Echo words, or effective repetition of key words in a paragraph, reinforce the key point. This repetition, instead of being redundant, reminds the reader of the paragraph topic and the relevance of details. Notice the echoes in the paragraph presented next.

Workplace Application—Echoes

P   T

There are **excellent sampling procedures** in place for final product. They run **extensive laboratory analyses** on samples from the test hopper in order to grade materials as prime or off-grade. **Additional sampling and testing** are conducted on the railcar retain **sample** at the time of shipment. Three compartments **are sampled** from each railcar for melt flow index, with one **analysis** run on each **sample**. **Additional tests** are also run on a composite **sample** from the railcar.

Of course, too many echoes can become redundant—saying the same thing several times. Be sure to use only relevant details and vary your word choice.

Logical Chain

Studies show that readers can follow even the most complex technical information more easily if sentences move from known information to new information. In other words, clearly organized paragraphs build a logical chain—one link at a time. Imagine this progression:

Known ⟶ new. Known ⟶ new. Known ⟶ new . . .

In the next paragraph, each sentence builds on the information presented in the sentence before.

Workplace Application—Logical Chain

I propose this well should be checked for scaling tendencies to determine **if some remedial work** should be performed to improve production. **If no remedial work** is indicated, temporary abandonment should be considered while **other options** are explored. **These options** include

plug and abandonment, checking for other potential producing zones, or converting to a salt water disposal well
to serve both the United and Excellent production areas.

Practice: Scrambled Paragraph

The following sentences are not in their original paragraph order.
Based on the clues you draw from logical order, transitions, and
echo words, rearrange the sentences into their original order. (The
original order appears after the Paragraph Revision Practice.)

1. For example, notifications of additional employee earnings
   and expenses paid by our field offices are not received until
   after December 31.

2. Therefore, additional liabilities are probable, thus justifying
   AMENDED returns.

3. Of the $431,066.23 refund requested, please leave $50,000
   in reserve for future 2005 tax liabilities to be reported on
   amended returns.

4. As a result, determination of tax protection requirements and
   liabilities cannot be fully completed until after all earnings data
   has been received and analyzed.

5. As the company is a worldwide enterprise and many of our
   employees travel extensively on both temporary and long-
   term assignments, the knowledge of employee Federal and
   State taxable earnings is not available at year end.

WORKSPACE

Practice: Paragraph Revision

Revise the following paragraph to create a stronger key point and make the details clearer with action steps:

> Attached (to the District copy only) is a listing of the active record (Facility/Plant) for respective Districts. This listing needs to be reviewed for status changes and/or corrections which should be reported by Form 6050 in accordance with MCM-515, Topic D-2. Upon completion of your review, advise Data Control Group (Ann Clark, Room 111) by letter and attach any Form 6050 you prepared. Also, send a copy of your letter to Joan Johnson, Data Center. The review should be completed and the Data Control Group advised by June 18, 200_.

WORKSPACE

Original Order of Scrambled Paragraph (see page 93)

> **(3)** Of the $431,066.23 refund requested, please leave $50,000 in reserve for future 2005 tax liabilities to be reported on amended returns. **(5)** As the company is a worldwide enterprise and many of our employees travel extensively on both temporary and long-term assignments, the knowledge of employee Federal and State taxable earnings is not available at year end. **(1)** For example, notifications of additional employee earnings and expenses paid by our field offices are not received until after December 31. **(4)** As a result, determination of tax protection requirements and liabilities cannot be fully completed until after all earnings data has been received and analyzed. **(2)** Therefore, additional liabilities are probable, thus justifying AMENDED returns.

Hooking Paragraphs Together

These same techniques—logical order, transitions, echoes, and logical chains—are also effective in creating links between paragraphs. Acting like hooks that connect railcars, these paragraph transitions are smooth when:

- The topic sentence clearly relates to and advances the main idea of the document.

- Standard transition words appear in the topic sentence to hook it to the preceding paragraph.

- Key words from the preceding paragraph are echoed in the topic sentence of the next.

Of course, to build such a logical structure, having a clear map is essential. Even a rough plan that you create before actually writing will help. Making ideas clear to your readers is impossible until *you* know what you are going to say.

OPENING AND CLOSING

The opening and closing paragraphs in any document are extremely important because they may be the only part of the document your readers read. Most people say they usually look at the first paragraph to learn what the document is about and the last paragraph to learn what to do and by when (see Figure 4-3).

Your opening paragraph should:

- Identify the business issue or problem.

- State the purpose and/or main idea (solution).

Your closing paragraph should:

- Restate the main idea.

- State the specific action to be taken and the due date, if possible.

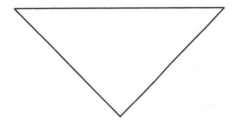

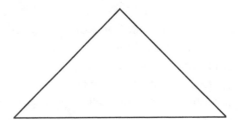

| **Issue** | I am responding to your search for a technical writer as advertised in the *Daily News*. . . . |
| **Purpose** | This letter will summarize my background and qualifications. |

| **Main Idea** | Once you have have had an opportunity to review the enclosed resume, . . . |
| **Action** | I will call next week to see if we can meet in person to further discuss my qualifications. |

| **Problem** | Eunice Matthews has sent me 37 different letters which Customer Service currently has set up on word processing. |
| **Main Idea** | This large number raises several concerns about consistency. |

| **Main Idea** | I am now asking for your help in addressing the letters situation. . . . |
| **Action** | By March 3, would each of you please prepare the following: . . . |

Figure 4-3. Opening and closing paragraphs

Opening and Closing Style

Most writers rely on stock openings and closings to save time and to feel confident their style is appropriate. But try to avoid the tired phrases that often begin and end letters, memos, and e-mail. Instead, choose phrases with a modern, human voice.

Write openings that sound like a professional conversation.

Instead of the old-fashioned:	*Try the modern:*
Please be advised that your proposal has been approved.	Your proposal has been approved.
In reference to your letter dated . . .	Thank you for your January 6, 200_ letter.
This memo is in reply to your request . . .	As you requested, . . .
The purpose of this report is to analyze . . .	This report analyzes . . .
As per our telephone conversation . . .	As we discussed . . .
Enclosed please find a list of . . .	The enclosed list . . .
Herein attached is a spreadsheet . . .	The attached spreadsheet . . .
This will acknowledge your letter of . . .	We received your letter . . .
We regret (or are pleased) to inform you that . . .	Unfortunately . . . Congratulations . . .
In your letter dated June 17, it was stated . . .	Your June 17 letter stated . . .

Write closings that sound like a natural call to action.

Instead of:	*Try:*
Old-fashioned Hoping to hear from you in the affirmative, I am . . .	**Modern** I hope you agree to . . .
Cliché Enclosed you will find a self-addressed, stamped envelope for your convenience.	**Fresh** Please return the form in the enclosed envelope.
Negative Please do not hesitate to call.	**Positive** Please call . . .
Formal Your cooperation in this matter will be greatly appreciated.	**Natural** Thank you for your help.
Vague Please respond at your earliest convenience.	**Precise** Please return the form before June 1.

Writing (sidebar)

Practice: Revising Openings and Closings

Rewrite these openings and closings to be more concise and effective:

1. It has come to my attention that an overcharge was made in December on my account of $25.00.

2. We have referred your letter of November 15 to our Legal Department, and they have advised us that you are entitled to full coverage.

3. Thanks in advance for your cooperation in this request for more current statistics.

4. Your assistance in resolving this problem before December 31 is greatly appreciated.

5. As per our conversation of Monday, May 26, 200_, in regard to the aforementioned project, it is my wish that you proceed.

CREATING VISUAL CLUES

Traditional paragraph style creates a box—one sentence after another with either a five-space indentation or no indentation at the beginning. New technology allows us to create much more reader-friendly paragraphs.

- Open lists that look like an **I** or **T**
- Columns for comparisons
- Inserted graphics with meaty captions

These modern paragraphs still meet the traditional definition of a paragraph: "A paragraph is a group of sentences explaining one idea."

Workplace Application— Traditional vs. Open Layout

The open format in paragraphs helps readers grasp information more easily. As Chapter 3 suggested, lists with white space and headings open up seemingly dense text. The logical relationships then take shape, just as they did after a supervisor suggested revising the memo from the original in Figure 4-4 to the revised in Figure 4-5. What did the writer change to improve clarity and readability?

Date: 12/16/0_

To: Manager

From: Maintenance Clerk

Subject: Kit Alternatives

The original Log Plan for the controller used 6 Regional offices for the Kit distribution centers due to the high cost of the Third Program stated below. The 6 Regional Kits would cost $_____ dollars. But, one exposure in regards to that plan was establishing only 6 sites for Kits would be insufficient saturation of spare parts in the field.

Attached are three alternative Kit distribution cost analyses. The first program would consist of 12 centers, located at key Air Freight Hub Distribution sites at a cost of $_____. Second program consists of 14 centers, located at _____. To establish this program would be $_____. The third program is the most costly at $_____. They would be distributed to all 129 Service Centers forecasted in the Maintenance Plan.

Figure 4-4. Original memo—traditional paragraph layout

Date: 12/16/0_

To: Manager

From: Maintenance Clerk

Subject: Kit Alternatives

The original Log Plan for the controller used 6 Regional offices for the Kit distribution centers due to the high cost of the Third Program stated below in "Alternatives." But establishing only 6 sites for Kits could mean that not enough spare parts would reach the field.

Original Plan:

   6 Regional kits = $

Alternatives:

   First Program = $

      Consists of 12 centers, located at Key Air
      Freight Hub Distribution sites.

   Second Program = $

      Consists of 14 centers, located at 6 Regional
      offices plus 8 additional Zones.

   Third Program = $

      Consists of all 129 Service Centers forecasted in the
      Maintenance Plan.

You will find attached cost analyses of the three Alternative programs for Kit distribution.

Figure 4-5. Revised memo—open paragraph layout

Practice: Paragraph Formatting

Legal notices to consumers often pack as much information into a paragraph as possible. Besides being very reader-*unfriendly*, such notices seem designed to hide meaning. Reformat the disclosure clause in Figure 4-6 to open up the visually packed paragraph and clarify the terms of subscriber privacy.

DISCLOSURE. The Cable Act allows us to collect personally identifiable information and to disclose it to a third party only if (a) you consent in advance in writing or electronically; (b) disclosure is necessary to render cable service and other services we provide to you and related business activities; (c) disclosure is required pursuant to a court order and you are notified of such order; or (d) for mailing lists as described below. The Cable Act requires us to inform you of the nature, frequency, and purpose of any disclosure which may be made of such information, including the identification of the types of persons to whom the disclosure may be made. We may make your records available to employees, agents and contractors to install, market, provide, or audit cable service and to measure viewership and customer satisfaction on each occasion access is needed for the specific job at hand. Access for these purposes is routine, and does not occur with any specific frequency. We may also occasionally release our customer list to a consumer research organization to conduct market research for services provided and programs shown by the cable system. Access for these purposes occurs when needed and not with any specific frequency. Further, we make our customer list available each month to an independent billing house to send bills, to provide our customers information relating to their cable service or other services provided by us, and to provide our customers information relating to other products and services offered by third parties; to distributors each month for sending program guides; to programmers for marketing and promotions of their services carried on our system; to programmers and outside auditors to check our records whenever such audits are required, as needed; to attorneys and accountants on a continuous basis as necessary to render service to the company; to potential purchasers in connection with a system sale which occurs only at the time such sale is contemplated; to franchising authorities to demonstrate compliance with the franchise when requested; to mailing services as needed for system-related mailings to customers; and to collection services if required to collect past due bills at such time as bills are submitted for collection. Where utilized, customer information also is disclosed to our bill payment lock box service each month as necessary for processing customer payments.

Figure 4-6. Reader-unfriendly notice

Writing

> Computers have changed how paragraphs look. The modern "paragraph" may very well be a graphic with a caption that interprets the data.

INTEGRATING TEXT AND VISUALS

Readers process information in different ways: visually by reading words, auditorially through hearing, kinesthetically by handling objects or doing tasks, and holistically through seeing how the whole relates to the parts. Traditional text has appealed to only one of those learning styles—the visual learner. However, computers make it possible to integrate text and visuals, thus helping holistic learners process information more effectively.

Besides being sensitive to learning styles, good writers understand that some information is simply clearer if laid out in a graphic form. But interpreting the details with a complete caption – or strong topic sentence – is still important.

Figure 4-7 shows how the same data has greater impact as a bar chart than as text. The text includes more historical explanation, but the visual "tells" the story more dramatically.

A. Text

The number of school districts continues to decline. In 1914, the state had 5,889 school districts—the largest number since statehood when schools were located within walking distance of every child. Between 1947 and 1965, almost 3,300 schools were annexed or consolidated. Incentives provided in 1990 fostered renewed interest in consolidation, reducing the number of school districts as of January 2002 to 543.

B. Visual

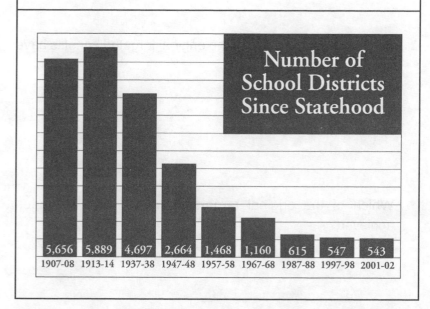

Number of School Districts Since Statehood

| 5,656 | 5,889 | 4,697 | 2,664 | 1,468 | 1,160 | 615 | 547 | 543 |
| 1907-08 | 1913-14 | 1937-38 | 1947-48 | 1957-58 | 1967-68 | 1987-88 | 1997-98 | 2001-02 |

Figure 4-7. Text versus visual impact. *Source:* Oklahoma State Department of Education, *The Progress of Education Reform, Volume 7,* June 2002.

Practice: Integrating Text and Visuals

If a chart or table is the best way to organize details clearly, the title and caption should state the key point. With only a title, the reader must analyze the data. The table in Figure 4-8 lacks such interpretation. Read through all the sections and answer these questions:

1. For **Inventory**, which of the original targeted benefits have been achieved?

Which of the original targeted benefits have not been achieved?

2. For **Purchasing**, which of the original targeted benefits have been achieved?

Which of the original targeted benefits have not been achieved?

3. Write a title that more fully describes the idea being presented in MIS Report—Table 1.

4. Write a caption that summarizes in a few sentences how much the new MIS system has achieved in reaching the targeted benefits for Inventory and Purchasing (#1 and #2).

MIS Report—Table 1 Expected Benefits vs. Results		
Application	**Original Target Benefits**	**Results to Date**
1. Inventory	• Reduction of unplanned downtime • Reduction in emergency delivery costs • Elimination of significant writedowns • Indentification of redundant inventory in warehouses • Elimination of obsolete inventory • Reduction of inventory levels, managing min./max.	• Inventory levels have been reduced at some locations due to use of min./max. quantities and re-order analysis programs. • Roof bolts and other bulk items are more closely managed; communication between warehouse/purchasing managers has opened up since installation of the MIS, and they have actively exchanged ideas on procedures and common problems across mines and regions. • Reliability (data integrity) and responsiveness of the MIS is improved over prior system. • Reorder analysis has had major improvement over the prior system. MIS has been flexible, usable, and allows the mine to proactively manage inventory. • Manual General Ledger recording of inventory activity has been eliminated.
2. Purchasing	• Better control over the purchasing function • Monitor vendor performance better • Utilize buying power to reduce price • Take advantage of discounts on payables • Fewer calls to vendors • Online purchase approvals, reduction of paper and time spent	• Controls definitely improved as a result of MIS—delivery of goods not authorized without a PO number. • Automatic order generation from reorder analysis. • Vendor analysis provided with interface between purchasing and accounts payable. • Vendor price history is kept in the MIS (history is just now building usefulness). • Phone pricing and ordering still occurs; however, PO can be set up on-line and given to vendor right then. • Productivity improved in procurement through automated purchasing paperwork and vendor performance reporting. • Discounts on purchases almost always taken due to invoices getting into MIS much faster than before. • Paper flow is reduced by on-line requisitions. (Even though it is not at full potential, it has also improved control over approvals.)

Figure 4-8. Integrating text and visuals

Editing

Potential Problems	Strategies
Words that make reading difficult	Remember your audience by: ■ Eliminating or defining jargon for lay readers; ■ Preferring plain English; ■ Choosing an informal, personal style
Complex or unclear words	Avoid pompous vocabulary and vague, abstract terms.
Wordiness, redundancy	Be concise and direct by: ■ Pruning wordy phrases; ■ Choosing action verbs; ■ Preferring active to passive verbs; ■ Eliminating hedgers and empty sentence beginnings.
Careless word choice	Choose words that say exactly what you mean. Always run spellcheck. Then proofread.

Editing

CHAPTER 5—EDITING

Editing

EDITING FOR CLEAR STYLE

Malcolm Forbes, founder and editor-in-chief of *Forbes Magazine*, offered this great advice: "***Be natural—write the way you talk.*** Imagine [the reader] sitting in front of you—what would you say to him? . . . The acid test—read your letter out loud when you're done. You might get a shock—but you'll know for sure if it sounds natural." [*emphasis in the original*]

Too often, workplace writing lacks personality—it sounds like no *person* has written it and no *person* is addressed. In trying to sound professional, some writers mimic the same voice or tone—impersonal, complex, and harder to read than necessary. In editing, you begin the re-visioning—or looking again at what you've written—that allows you to change a reader-unfriendly style into a plain style that has a Voice—the sound of you communicating with your readers. To begin rewriting for an effective voice, ask, "Is my style precise, appropriate, clear, and concise?"

Precise

Choose words that say what you mean.

Not: The Information Services manager who said, "Our goal is to create a huge data suppository."

Choose words with precise, vivid connotations.

Interest rates *ballooned* for two reasons. To further *cement* their existing relationship . . .

Appropriate

Replace high-sounding words with plain English.

He advised . . .
He indicated . . . ⎫ He said . . .
He notified . . . ⎭

Use " you" and "I."

This writer has been notified by your office that . . . ➤ As you told me . . .

Clear

Beware of vague, abstract words.

The tank is almost full. ➤ The tank contains 14 gallons, with a 16-gallon capacity.

Use pronouns that clearly refer to a noun.

This proves the breakdown occurred because . . . ➤ This series of events proves the breakdown occurred because . . . .

Concise

Cross out redundant phrases.

In the amount of $10.00 ➤ $10.00

Never use several words when one word will do.

With respect to ➤ about
In conjunction with ➤ with
In order to ➤ to

Resurrect strong verbs from derived nouns and adjectives.

Consideration ➤ consider
Decision ➤ decide
Accomplishment ➤ accomplish
Beneficial for ➤ benefits

Replace passive verbs by using the "Who does what" sentence pattern.

The decision was made by us. ➤ We decided . . .

Omit empty sentence beginnings such as "There" and "It."

There is overwhelming evidence that suggests . . . ➤ Overwhelming evidence suggests . . .

Self-Assessment Activity

Describe how you want to sound on paper. What voice *do* you and do you *not* want to project?

Do	*Don't*

POLISHING FOR PRECISION

Choose the words that say precisely what you intend.

Words carry two types of meaning:

■ **Denotation**, which is the literal or generally accepted meaning

■ **Connotation**, or the implied or associated meanings

For example, "leave" means to exit or go away from. So does "abandon," but the latter implies an emergency (the connotation). With both words you would no longer inhabit the same space (the denotation); however, if you "abandon," you leave quickly, not intending to return.

To choose the precise word, edit for the following:

■ **Exact Connotations**—Choose words that carry the precise meaning you intend. Gain as much mileage from your words as you can. For example, do you mean "meet" or "gather" or "confer"? Is it a "conference" or an "event" or a "symposium" or a "presentation"?

■ **Fresh Vocabulary**—Choose interesting words. We tend to rely on the same overused vocabulary of about 600 words. Dust off your larger working vocabulary. Instead of "provide," try "give" or "send" or "offer" or "mail" or "ship" or "explain" or . . .

■ **Unanticipated Meaning**—Do **NOT** use unfamiliar words you discover in the thesaurus. If a word is not part of your working vocabulary, do not use it. It will sound unnatural, plus you can make an embarrassing error. One banking memo that analyzed a new federal banking regulation began, "This is to explain the prophylactic regulation." Right meaning; wrong connotation.

DETERMINING APPROPRIATENESS

Traditional writing valued one style—the formal. Complex vocabulary, elaborate sentences, and strict rules marked the educated person. But such complexity assumed that readers had the time and inclination to enjoy text, savoring the development of arguments and learned vocabulary. Some still do. But most modern workplace readers prefer a more direct, clear style to ornate complexity.

In interviewing Ernest Hemingway, a reporter said he had heard Hemingway had a hard time with a chapter of For Whom the Bell Tolls. Hemingway said that, yes, it required revising. The reporter asked how many revisions, and Hemingway answered, "37." Asked what the problem was, Papa replied, "Getting the words right."

Most workplace writers do not have that kind of time to master just the right word. But they should choose their words wisely to gain clarity and impact.

Thus, one style does not fit all documents. In editing, you need to decide what words will be appropriate for this audience on this occasion. Some documents will be formal; others should be informal. Some will omit personal references; others will focus on "you"—the reader, customer, coworker. Therefore, edit your text to meet the needs of your different readers by observing the following guidelines.

Be Sensitive to Jargon

Jargon is the shared vocabulary of any group—a profession, a company, a social club, a family. Who determines the fine line between a precise, professional vocabulary (appropriate jargon) and meaningless verbiage? Your readers. For experts (or members of the group), jargon expresses complex ideas very clearly and concisely. However, jargon excludes non-experts. When used with the wrong audience, it confuses and divides. You will use jargon in the workplace. However, be careful.

Of course, we have no trouble recognizing someone else's jargon. We've all trudged through an incoherent insurance policy or legal document. The trend, however, is away from using jargon. These days, the professions, insurance companies, and government are rewriting documents in a readable style to be more customer-friendly—and clear.

Workplace Application—Promissory Note

Old: "No extension of time for payment, or delay in enforcement hereof, nor any renewal of this note, with or without notice, shall operate as a waiver of any rights hereunder or release the obligation of any maker, guarantor, endorser or any other accommodation party."

New: "We can delay enforcing any of our rights without losing them."

Workplace Application—Jargon

These statements were supposed to communicate professionally. See if you can translate each into plain English.

Walter Kaufmann elaborated on the social implications of proliferating jargon: "Men love jargon. It is so palpable, tangible, visible, audible; it makes so obvious what one has learned; it satisfies the craving for results. It is impressive for the uninitiated. It makes one feel that one belongs. Jargon divides men into Us and Them."

1. Witnesseth: That parties to these presents, each in consideration of the undertakings, promises and agreements on the part of the other herein contained, have undertaken, promised, and agreed and do hereby undertake, promise and agree, each for itself, its successors and assigns, as follows:

2. *A bulletin sent to parents described a new Houston education program:*

   "Our school's cross-graded, multi-ethnic, individualized learning program is designed to enhance the concept of an open-ended learning program with emphasis on a continuum of multi-ethnic, academically enriched learning, using the identified intellectually gifted child as the agent or director of his own learning. Major emphasis is on cross-graded, multi-ethnic learning with the main objective being to learn respect for the uniqueness of a person."

   (One parent responded to this bulletin: "Dear Principal: I have a college degree, speak two foreign languages, and know four Indian dialects. I've attended a number of county fairs and three goat ropings but I haven't the faintest idea as to what the hell you are talking about.")

3. *From an address on economic and financial management:*

   "A slow-up of the slowdown is not as good as an upturn of the downcurve, but it is better than either a speedup of the slowdown or a deepening of the downcurve— and it suggests the climate is right for an adjustment of the readjustment.

   "Turning to unemployment, we find a definite decrease in the rate of increase— which shows there is a letting up of the letdown. If the slowdown should speed up, the decrease in the rate of increase of unemployment would turn into an increase in the rate of decrease of unemployment.

   "We expect a leveling-off—referred to on Wall Street as bumping along rock bottom—sometime this winter. This will be followed by a gentle pickup, then a faster pickup, a slow-down of the pickup, and finally a leveling off in the spring."

4. He was proceeding to install pedestrian heads on mast arm poles at the southwest corner.

5. As lit capacity is eliminated from the market and the long-haul carriers bring their guns to bear on the metro marketplace, which will provide on-ramps to their high capacity cores, we predict an uptick in the competitive telecom marketplace will unfold.

Analysis: How did you react to this jargon? What did you think as you read the statements? How would (or did) you respond? It is easy to criticize other people's jargon, but we are comfortable with our own. Others react to our jargon just as we did to the preceding statements. (See Figure 5-1.)

Prefer the Plain Style

Although not exactly jargon, an inflated vocabulary of "business-ese" has become a specialized language of its own. Generally, this style is too formal and wordy. Growing out of a Latinate vocabulary, it produces an overblown voice that can easily be pared to more concise, clear statements. The plain style, on the other hand, is clearer and easier to read. It is also appropriate.

There is nothing wrong with big words. In fact, a rich vocabulary helps you find the word with the precise meaning you need. However, choose the familiar term instead of the formal *if* the two do not differ in meaning (see Table 5-1).

Figure 5-1. Writing to impress versus to express. Cartoon by Jeff MacNelly. Courtesy of Tribune Media Services, Inc. All rights reserved. Reprinted with permission.

Table 5-1. Choose the Familiar Form

Formal	Familiar
apprise	mention
ascertain	determine, find out
avail oneself	use
cognizant of	aware of, recognize
commence	begin
contingent upon	depend on
deem	think
discontinue	stop
endeavor	try
enhance	improve
facilitate	help, ease
finalize	complete
forward	send
generate	create
indicate	say, suggest
initiate	start, begin
interface	meet
per	as, by, according to
presently	now
prior to	before
provide	send, give, offer
render	make, give
subsequent to	after
transmit	send, give
transpire	happen
utilize	use

"It's been a long time since I've heard someone say, 'I can't understand what he's saying; he must be highly intelligent.'"
—Douglas Mueller

Practice: Formal Style

In plain English, what were the writers of the following statements talking about?

1. The troop leader told his men that "the movement to the new station will be implemented by means of wheeled, gas-operated vehicles."

2. Illumination is required to be extinguished on these premises.

3. This construction will encourage the use of leg power for vertical pedestrian circulation.

4. Packing is always an issue, whether in the air or ground, you must have enough for your expedition to accommodate your necessities.

5. If you should have any questions or comments, please feel free to contact myself at your convenience. Once again thanks for your cooperation and support. It has been a pleasure dealing with your organization and our relationship shall continue to strengthen.

Workplace Application—Using a Plain Style

The original and revised letters in Figure 5-2 and Figure 5-3 reveal what happens when the plain style replaces the legalistic, formal style. Both also use jargon, but the plain style in the revised version minimizes it. Though these letters are not identical in content, notice the improvement in clarity and customer focus.

May 30, 200_

Oil Company Inc.
P.O. Box 1234
City, ST 46387

ATTENTION: Ms. Ann Autry

Re: Oil #748750
     Property Description
     Production County, ST

Dear Ann:

Further to our phone conversation this date, please provide us with a copy of the BRA Decision Letter whereby transferring the subject lease to minimum royalty status. Said lease was earned under Farmin between Service Oil and Gas Corporation (Farmoutee) and Oil Company Inc. (Farmoutor), dated November 9, 200_.

As confirmed by our phone conversation it is our understanding that Oil Company Inc., record title owner of the subject lease, will be responsible for any minimum royalty which might become due under the said lease.

To evidence this understanding and to eliminate any question relative to the above, please sign and date at the bottom and return one copy to the attention of the undersigned.

Thank you for your assistance in this matter and should you have any questions, please do not hesitate to contact me.

Sincerely,

Western Oil, Inc.

Thomas Smith

Thomas Smith
Landman—Land Department

TLS/abc

Figure 5-2. Original formal style letter

July 15, 200_

Oil Company Inc.
P.O. Box 1234
City, ST 46387

ATTENTION: Mr. Bob Netter

Re: Oil #648930—Farmout Agreement
     Property Description
     Production County, ST

Dear Bob:

In our letter of June 27, 200_, we requested a copy of the Bureau of Resource Adjustment
Notice transferring the referenced lease to minimum royalty status. However, we have not
received a reply.

In order to complete our file, we will need additional information from you as Record Title
Owner. For your convenience we have enclosed a copy of our letter of May 27, 200_.
Please sign and date at the bottom of that letter and return one copy to me.

Thank you for your cooperation in this matter. If you have any questions or if we can be of
any assistance, please feel free to contact me.

Sincerely,

Western Oil, Inc.

Thomas Smith

Thomas Smith
Landman—Land Department

TLS/abc
enclosure

Figure 5-3. Revised plain style letter

Practice: Editing for an Inflated Style

Translate the inflated letter shown in Figure 5-4 into plain English. Chapter 7, "Practice," contains additional documents to edit for clarity, appropriateness, and conciseness.

Dear David:

Enclosed please find the above referenced written Consent for your execution. It is required that we request your signature, your obtainment of the signature of Patterson O. Smithfield, and the subsequent restoration of the original document to myself. I will then be responsible for the transmission of this Consent to the remainder of the Board of Directors for their respective approbations.

Figure 5-4. Editing for inflated style

EDITING WORKSPACE

Use a "You" Focus

A "you" focus increases the readability of a document by pulling your reader into the conversation. That means that you speak directly to the reader, prefering "you" to "I" or "we." In writing a draft, we tend to focus on "I": what I did and what I want. In editing, refocus the text on your reader, "you." The original and revised versions of the letter in Figure 5-5 and Figure 5-6 show how the focus on "you" makes the tone more direct and personal. The revised version is also shorter and uses less jargon.

Workplace Application—"We" vs. "You" Focus

Harrison Lane
1234 South Houston
City, ST 87654

Dear Mr. Lane:

Thank you for notifying us of the death of Opal Lane.

To enable us to issue a transfer order reflecting the new ownership of the interest formerly credited to the deceased, please furnish the items listed in number 1 or 2 below or the Affidavit listed in number 3.

1. If the Will was probated in the State of Texas, we will need a copy of the certified Will and Order Admitting it to probate in Texas, along with Letters Testamentary.

2. If the Will was probated in a state other than Texas, we will need authenticated copies (three-way certificate) of the Will and the Order Admitting the Will to Probate filed in the deed records of the County shown in the caption of this letter, along with Letters Testamentary. Excerpts from Texas statutes affecting lands in Texas devised by foreign Will are enclosed for your information.

3. If there was no will or if probate procceedings will not be held, please complete the enclosed Affidavit of Heirship, giving special attention to paragraphs 9, 10, and 15. We will then transfer the interest according to the Affidavit of Heirship, based on the Texas Laws of Descent and Distribution.

Please provide the Social Security or Tax Identification Numbers of the heirs, along with their current addresses. A return envelope has been enclosed for your convenience. If there is a surviving spouse, please advise if the interests were community or separate property.

Sincerely,

Legal Accounting

Figure 5-5. Original letter—focus on "we"

Harrison Lane
1234 South Houston
City, ST 87654

Dear Mr. Lane:

Thank you for notifying us of the death of Opal Lane. We will issue a transfer order to the new owners when you send the items listed in number 1, 2, or 3 below:

1. **If the Will was probated in Texas**, send us a copy of the recorded Will and Order Admitting the Will to probate along with Letters Testamentary.

2. **If the Will was probated in a state other than Texas**, you must gather certified copies of the Will, the Order Admitting the Will to probate, and the Letters Testamentary filed in the deed records of Simpson County. We are enclosing excerpts of Texas statutes that apply when the will is probated in a state other than Texas.

3. **If there was no Will or if probate proceedings will not be held**, complete the enclosed Affidavit of Heirship. Please give special attention to paragraphs 9, 10, and 15. The transfer of interest will be made according to the Affidavit based on Texas Laws of Descent and Distribution.

Please provide the Social Security or Tax Identification numbers and current addresses of the heirs. If there is a surviving spouse, we need to know if the royalty interests were community or separate property.

If you have questions, call me at (908) 555-1212 or write to the above address.

Sincerely,

Legal Accounting

Figure 5-6. Revised letter—focus on "you"

Practice: Improving the "You" Focus

Revise the letter in Figure 5-7 to improve its "you" attitude. Instead of focusing on what "I need," emphasize what "you" [the customer] can do to achieve the results "you" want. Your revisions will also improve the letter's customer focus.

July 30, 200_

Walter Lee
5489 River Lane
City, ST 78957

Mr. Lee,

In order to add Jamie to your account I need you both to please sign the enclosed signature card. I need you to sign in three places, once on the front by your name and twice on the back by the highlighted X's. Then I just need Jamie's signature one time on the front of the card by the highlighted X. I have also provided a postage-paid envelope for you to return the signature card at your earliest convenience.

If you have any questions or concerns please feel free to call. I have included my business card with the branch number. Thank you.

Sincerely,

Customer Service Representative

Figure 5-7. Improving the "you" focus

WORKSPACE

Prefer Positive to Negative

Studies show that readers process positive statements more quickly and accurately than they do identical information stated negatively. A positive statement is also more compelling. Therefore, you should replace negative phrases with positive, if you can. For example:

Negative	*Positive*
Please do not hesitate to call.	Please call.
If you cannot find the information before Monday, it won't matter.	Waiting to find the information on Monday would be fine.

Workplace Application—Negative

The disclaimer in Figure 5-8 appears on a law firm's Web site, the purpose of which, presumably, is to attract clients. Legally the firm must state that the Web site does not contain legal advice or constitute an agreement to represent a client. However, the negative language could certainly block a potential client's interest.

Disclaimer

The material on this Web site is provided for informational purposes, and neither Law nor its attorneys make any guarantee that the material is kept up to date or is correct or complete. . . . No attorney of Law will represent a client in any jurisdiction in which that attorney is not licensed to practice law . . .

The information presented is NOT intended as a substitute for specific legal advice or opinions, and the transmission of this information is NOT intended to create an attorney-client relationship between sender and receiver. . . .

While we would like to hear from you, we cannot represent you until we know that doing so will not create a conflict of interest. Please do not send us any information about any matter . . .

In the event that this communication is not in conformity with the regulations of any state, this law firm is not willing to accept representation based on this communication.

Figure 5-8. Negative tone

Sounds like the firm in Figure 5-8 can't do much and doesn't want new clients. Compare that negative tone to the disclaimer in Figure 5-9 that accomplishes the same goal—legal protection for another firm—with a more positive tone.

Workplace Application—Positive

Please contact any of our attorneys or call one of our four offices to initiate possible representation by Legal Partners. A standard conflict-of-interest procedure will be followed to ensure the integrity of client interests, with follow-up made by the attorney whose expertise is best suited for counsel in your matter.

Legal Partners publishes this and other business communications for informational purposes only. This communication does NOT substitute for specific legal advice or opinions. Further, the publication of this information is NOT intended to create an attorney-client relationship.

Figure 5-9. Positive tone

Choose Unbiased Language

Avoiding stereotyping through word choice is a relatively recent communication concern. As the ideas of traditionally male and female occupations have changed, our sense of appropriate language use has also changed. Why distract a reader from your message through a poor word choice? The following guidelines suggest graceful ways to avoid sexual reference without cluttering your writing with awkward "he/she," "gentleperson," and "humankind" alternatives.

Avoid "man-words" when referring to all people.

Instead of	*Use*
mankind	humanity, people
If a man completes the job . . .	If a person completes the job . . .
man-made	synthetic, manufactured
manpower	workers, workforce
businessman	executive, manager, owner
congressman	member of Congress
salesman	salesperson, clerk
fireman, policeman	firefighter, police officer
chairman	chair, chairperson

Use nonsexist pronouns.

■ Choose gender-neutral words when referring to all people.

The average man drives his car . . .	*The average person drives a car . . .*

■ Use the plural form.

The average person drives his car . . .	*Most people drive their cars . . .*

■ Use a neutral pronoun.

When a consumer looks for a bargain, he may buy . . .	*When looking for a bargain, one may buy . . . or*
	. . . you may buy . . . or
	. . . he or she may buy . . .

■ Use a passive rather than an active verb.

Every employee participates in the health plan. He should pick up the forms . . .	*Every employee participates in the health plan. The forms may may be picked up . . .*

Avoid sexual stereotyping in addressing correspondence.

■ Use the reader's name whenever possible:

Dear Mr. Smith:
Dear Ms. Wong:

The courtesy title Ms. is now widely accepted and solves the irrelevant question of a woman's marital status.

■ Use a neutral term when the sex of the reader is unknown:

Dear Executive:
Dear Manager:

■ Begin the letter without a salutation:

Simpson Hams, Inc.
105 Main Street
Sussex, Virginia 10007

Please send me a catalogue and price list for your products . . .

INCREASING CLARITY

Choose Specific and Concrete Words

Remember that words lower on the Ladder of Abstraction are clearer (see Chapter 4). For example, "Vigorous physical exercise at an early time is an excellent way to start the day" can be made more specific by saying, "Fifty pushups before breakfast can start the day right."

Practice: Clarity

Rewrite each of the following sentences so that it expresses the same idea in specific rather than abstract terms:

1. The cost of the equipment is too high.

2. The stock market is off.

3. What he needs is some kind of disciplinary treatment.

4. They had no one good way of doing things, and it took a lot of time getting things done.

Using analogies is an effective way to clarify abstract concepts. For example, an oil industry writer reshaped readers' understanding of the nature of rock by writing, "The global search for oil and gas is concentrated on sedimentary basins within hydrocarbon provinces where petroleum is stored below the surface in porous rocks, which act like giant sponges, known as reservoirs."

Check for Clear Pronoun Reference

<u>Pro</u>nouns take the place of nouns. Two pronouns—*this* and *which*—are often used carelessly to refer to an entire idea rather than to a particular noun. You can easily correct this "broad reference" by inserting a noun. For example,

Vague: The materials are scheduled to arrive next week. *This* will enable us to start production immediately.

Clearer: The materials are scheduled to arrive next week. *Their arrival* will enable us to start production immediately.

Vague: We expect to receive several requests, *which* should take awhile to complete.

Clearer: We expect to receive several requests, *a process which* should take awhile to complete.

Chapter 6, "Refining," includes more detailed information about pronouns and how to use them correctly.

Practice: Clear Pronoun Reference

First, circle every "this" in the following paragraph and see whether you can tie each one clearly to the noun it refers to. If not, edit the sentence to make the reference clear, either by changing the text or inserting the missing noun after "this."

> Implementing vendor specific validations will decrease error/rejection rates, necessitating fewer supplements and less provisioning/vendor communications. This will decrease both order cost and order time. As this is an intensive process, requiring thorough requirements analysis for each specific vendor, this will only be implemented for our major trading partners, the eight regional suppliers. This will also allow us greater applicability of our service agreements, as these are valid only for clean (error-free) orders.

WORKSPACE

CONSERVING WORDS

Another mark of the too-formal style is wordiness. Replacing deadwood phrases and choosing strong action verbs will improve the clarity and power of your sentences. Look for the following "red flag" phrases to remove 20 to 30 to sometimes 50 percent of the words—without loss of content.

Prune the Deadwood

Eliminate words that take up space without adding any meaning. They are like "deadwood" in shrubs—cluttering the plant without contributing substance.

Instead of	*Use*
Redundancies—phrases that repeat meaning	
in the amount of $10.59	$10.59
during the period of June 1 through July 15	from June 1 through June 15
located in **the state of** Texas	in Texas
red **in color**	red
the reason is because	because
Filler words—words that add no meaning	
in **the area of** Accounting	in Accounting
in **the field of** engineering	in engineering
on a daily **basis**	daily
with an efficient **manner**	efficiently
Preposition + noun + preposition —clumps of prepositional phrases that can be replaced with one word	
in order to	to
due to the fact that	because
in the event of	if
in regard to	about
in conjunction with	with
at the present time	now
at this point in time	now

Editing

> **"I want to get rid of the 'chatter' in my writing."**
> —An Administrative Assistant

Examples of Pruning Deadwood:

~~In an effort~~ to clarify our records, ~~we ask that you~~ provide additional information concerning your ownership. *please*

To clarify our records, please provide additional information concerning your ownership.

For ~~the purpose of~~ this report, the current compliance status is ~~the status~~ for ~~the six month period~~ October 1, 2003, through March 31, 2004.

For this report, the current compliance status is for October 1, 2003, through March 31, 2004.

Until ~~such time as~~ the necessary corrective documents are prepared ~~in order for~~ the *so* interest ~~to~~ be owned equally as intended, I have placed the interest of Sara Smith in *can* suspense and will continue to pay Sam Smith ~~individually~~ and Tom Smith individually.

Until the necessary corrective documents are prepared so the interest can be owned equally as intended, I have placed the interest of Sara Smith in suspense and will continue to pay Sam Smith and Tom Smith individually.

Strengthen Your Verbs

The power of the English language is in the verbs. Tap that power by replacing weak verbs, nouns, and adjectives with strong action verbs. Some examples include:

Instead of	*Use*
Nouns formed from verbs— frequently ending in *-tion, -sion, -son, -ment, -ance,* or *-ence.*	*Strong action verbs*
make a recommendation	recommend
make an investigation	investigate
make a comparison of	compare
make a decision to	decide
be in agreement with	agree
have a preference for	prefer
be in compliance with	comply

Author Jimmy Breslin, describing his anxiety about impending brain surgery: "If anything happens to my verbs, I'll be on home relief."

Editing

Instead of	*Use*
"to be" verb forms—sometimes paired with adjectives that hide a strong verb.	**Strong action verbs**
is beneficial to is persuasive is agreeable to	benefits persuades agrees
Passive voice—verbs in which the object is being acted upon (see "Prefer Active to Passive Verbs")	**Active voice**—Who does what?
A decision was made by the committee . . . The program is used to monitor . . . The form should be sent to . . .	The committee decided . . . The program monitors . . . Send the form to . . .
Empty openings—There and It	**Substance up front**
It is necessary that we begin to . . . There were thousands of spectators cheering . . . It is the recommendation of the committee that . . . There were several suggestions made during the meeting . . .	We must begin to . . . Thousands of spectators cheered . . . The committee recommends . . . Several suggestions were made . . .
Hedgers—phrases that limit responsibility	**Take a stand**
I think that the data shows . . . It is my opinion that we should change vendors . . .	The data shows . . . We should change vendors . . .

Examples of Editing for Strong Verbs:

If the issue can be identified with in the next two business days, we ~~will have the~~ *can* ~~opportunity to have~~ the interface adjusted to eliminate this issue.

If the issue can be identified within the next two business days, we can adjust the interface to eliminate this issue.

Recent payments may not ~~be~~ reflected ~~on~~ this statement.

This statement may not reflect recent payments.

Please ~~We ask that~~ payment ~~be made~~ immediately ~~on~~ these outstanding charges ~~in order~~ *return* to ~~get~~ your account ~~back~~ to a current status and to avoid further collection activity ~~from becoming necessary~~.

Please pay these outstanding charges immediately to return your account to a current status and to avoid further collection activity.

show ~~According to~~ our records ~~there are~~ outstanding charges ~~open~~ on your account number 758 ~~in the amount~~ of $35,802.54.

Our records show outstanding charges on your account number 758 of $35,802.54.

Workplace Application—Conciseness

Notice the difference in clarity and conciseness between the original and the revised versions in Figure 5-10 and Figure 5-11.

RE: Revised Letter to Chairman Jones on FERC Administrative Procedures

Attached for your review is a redraft of the December 20 letter initially intended to be sent to FERC Chairman Jones by Seaway's Jim Thompson regarding FERC administrative problems. It now incorporates the comments you provided as well as those of the other committee members. I hope you will take the opportunity to review the attached draft one more time and submit your comments to me. While there is no deadline set by our committee for a response, if you could supply something within the next two weeks, I would be most appreciative.

As you will recall the letter details problems, including the processing of orders by the Commission and the position taken by staff in rate cases and settlements, and offers solutions. Initially it was to serve as the basis for a meeting between Thompson and Jones. However, APP Director Kimberly Mason was made aware of the existence of this letter and, due to her interest in the matter, our final work product will be sent to her.

Attachment

Figure 5-10. Original memo—169 words

RE: Revised Letter to Chairman Jones on FERC Administrative Procedures

Please review and submit your comments within the next two weeks on the attached redraft of the December 20 letter from Seaway's Jim Thompson, Chairman of the Regulatory Affairs Committee, to FERC Chairman Jones. Incorporated are your comments and those of other committee members regarding the FERC administrative problems, including processing of orders by the Commission and the position taken by staff in rate cases and settlements.

This letter was to serve as the basis for a meeting between Thompson and Jones, but Kimberly Mason, APP Director, has shown an interest in this letter and our final work product will be sent to her.

Attachment

Figure 5-11. Revised version—104 words

Practice: Editing

Edit the memo in Figure 5-12 for conciseness and to give it a
human voice. Change any other readability problems you see.
You will find an edited version in Chapter 7, "Practice."

THE PURPOSE FOR THIS FORM IS TO ALLOW ACCOUNTING DEPARTMENT
PERSONAL TO SUBMIT TO THE EMPLOYEE SURVEY TASK FORCE SOME
SUGGESTIONS AND SOLUTIONS TO THE LISTED ATTENDANCE AND MORALE
CONCERNS. ALL INPUT RECEIVED BACK WILL BE TAKEN INTO CONSIDERA-
TION WHEN THE FINAL ACTION PLAN IS DRAWN UP AND SUBMITTED TO THE
EXECUTIVE COMMITTEE. IN ADDITION TO THIS FORM, THERE WILL BE SEV-
ERAL SMALLER MEETINGS SET UP TO RECEIVE ANY ADDITIONAL INPUT
(SEE ATTACHED SCHEDULE OF MEETINGS). THE DEADLINE FOR SUBMIT-
TING INPUT TO THE FINAL ACTION PLAN IS FEBRUARY 16.

[89 words]

Figure 5-12. Editing practice

EDITING WORKSPACE

Prefer Active to Passive Verbs

Passive verbs produce three unwanted results by:

- Adding unnecessary words;

- Robbing sentences of the force of *someone-doing-something;*

- Masking responsibility if the actor is omitted.

To make your sentences more effective and more concise, you should prefer active to passive verbs.

Active: George planned the retreat.

Passive: The retreat was planned by George.

The passive consists of this construction:

to be [is, was, were, been, being]   +   a verb ending in *–ed, -en,* or *–t*
                                                                    [loved, seen, hit]
auxiliary verb   +   **past participle**

plus a stated or implied "by" prepositional phrase

See the section on verb formation in Chapter 8, "Fundamentals." Study the transformation presented in Figure 5-13.

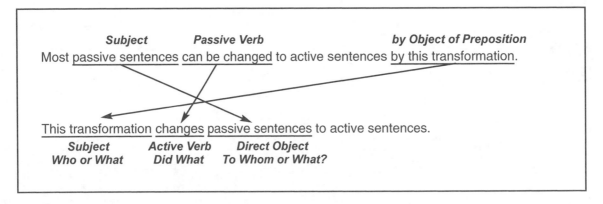

Figure 5-13. Passive-to-active transformation. The active verb form drops the helping verb and "by."

Example of Editing for Passive Verbs:

Once again you ~~will be~~ *must* ~~required to~~ attend the Defensive Driving Course and ~~it is ex-~~ ~~pected that~~ the information presented ~~to you will be applied and put~~ *apply* into daily practice.

Once again you must attend the Defensive Driving Course and apply the information presented in daily practice.

Practice: Passive to Active

Rewrite these passive sentences so that they have active verbs:

1. Checks presented for payment must be approved by GNMA.

2. A training manual or handout is provided for each participant.

3. The analyst is required to make determinations of the sample volume for initial use.

4. It was determined there was a need to educate and inform our employees about industry issues.

Practice: Editing for Strong Verbs

Edit these sentences to strengthen the verbs and increase the balance between active and passive:

1. The age range of children admitted to the Shelter is from birth to 17.

2. This was an occurrence that was unforeseen by the company and was outside of their control.

3. There are some overall concepts that represent a different approach than the current system.

4. In order to allow for an adequate evaluation, a sufficient amount of time is required.

5. Upon clicking on the icon with your remote, a second page with detailed information is displayed.

6. It seems we are faced with a serious issue.

7. Another reason for the improvement in Total Market Share was the increase in the industry attrition.

8. This section should be reviewed prior to the installation of the antenna.

9. Before proceeding, it is recommended the user(s) read and understand each section.

Practice: Editing

These sentences are clogged with deadwood and weak verbs. Eliminate the "chatter."

1. We are in receipt of a fifty dollar, $50., money order payable to General Utility Company.

2. My situation is that I have a request from Express Service for this service.

3. If there were any way to consolidate these accounts, month-end reconcilement would be greatly simplified.

4. I do feel that we need to continue the verification process that currently exists to ensure we are delivering an accurate instrument back to the field locations.

5. The survey was targeted at people who live in Austin, Texas, and information was gathered about their shopping habits.

6. There are a few customers whom we were unable to locate in our database through a name search.

7. Our company is a leader in the area of market research.

8. In order to sell effectively, it is important to understand your customers.

9. A notice will be distributed to all employees concerning the Summer Program.

More Practice Editing

The following paragraph is typical old-style, inflated text, laden with complex vocabulary, jargon, and wordy phrases. Revise it for clarity and conciseness:

Over the past few months, it has come to our attention that several of the district locations do not currently utilize these statements. Our understanding is that there are alternative sources of the same information (e.g., the Cumulative file) that many locations access through various computer extractions. Apparently, these extractions are providing the various locations with cost information sufficient to meet their needs. Accordingly, for the purpose of determining if issuance of the statements can be discontinued, we are asking that you review the usefulness of our Detail Cost statements to the Production Department. Removal of the requirements for issuance of such statements might possibly result in elimination of what appears to be a duplication of efforts on the part of our Department.   [123 words]

EDITING WORKSPACE

CHECKING FOR WORD DEMONS

Finally, check your spelling and word usage. Errors distract readers from your content and suggest you are careless. Beware of words that sound alike or are easily confused. You want to avoid the embarrassment of the manager whose proposal to move his department ended with, "The move will certainly increase the moral of the department." Also, be sure your dictionary is current. Language evolves as new words enter or old guidelines change. Using words correctly proves you are careful with your written product.

Some of these word demons include:

accent, ascent, assent. *Accent* implies speech emphasis or pronunciation. *Ascent* is "to climb," whereas *assent* means "to agree."

accept, except. *Accept* is a verb meaning "to agree to." Example: We *accept* your offer. *Except* involves leaving something out. Example: Everyone went *except* Joan.

access, excess. *Access* means "approaching" or "entering," whereas *excess* implies "more than enough" or "too much" of something. Examples: He gained *access* to the vault. He found an *excess* of old stock certificates.

advice, advise. *Advice* is a noun that means "giving one's opinion." Example: Here is my *advice*. *Advise* is the verb. Example: I *advise* you not to go. *Advise* has the –z sound.

affect, effect. *Affect* is a verb except in some professional jargon. Example: The change *affected* her attitude. *Effect* is usually a noun. Example: The *effect* of the change was dramatic. However, *effect* is sometimes used as a verb meaning "to create" or "produce." The good news *effected* great joy in Mudville.

allusion, illusion. *Allusion* is "an indirect reference to," whereas *illusion* is a "false vision." Examples: Her *allusion* to Homer suggested that the mythological gods were an *illusion*.

a lot, alot, allot. *A lot*, meaning "quite a bit," is always spelled with two words (not *alot*). Example: She had *a lot* of talent. *Allot* means "to set aside" or "apportion." He took his *allotted* share.

already, all ready. *Already* means "by this time." Example: The car had *already* passed the corner. *All ready* means "totally ready." Example: We are *all ready* to go.

amount, number. *Amount* is used with a bulk item. Example: She had a large *amount* of time on her hands. *Number* is used with countable items. Example: She had a *number* of days available.

and etc. Redundant. *Etc.* means "and others."

angel, angle. *Angel* is a heavenly being, whereas *angle* is where two points come together.

anxious, eager. *Anxious* comes from the root word *anxiety*. It implies worry. Example: He was *anxious* about her well-being. *Eager* means "looking forward to." Example: She was *eager* to get to work.

anyone, any one. *Anyone* is an indefinite pronoun. Example: Does *anyone* know when the meeting is? *Any one* refers to a particular one person or thing. Example: You can choose *any one* of the items in the drawing.

appraise, apprise. *Appraise* is an estimation of value. Example: The agent *appraised* the property too low. *Apprise* means "to tell." I will *apprise* you when the check arrives.

bad, badly. *Bad* is an adjective, the opposite of *good*. Example: He had a *bad* cold. *Badly* is the adverb. Example: He limped *badly* after the accident.

bare, bear. *Bare* is an adjective meaning "nude." *Bear* is either a large animal or a verb meaning "to carry." One new female employee got quite a response when she e-mailed her coworkers: "I have several questions and announcements about the library, so please *bare* with me."

between, among. Use *between* when referring to two persons or things and *among* when referring to more than two. Examples: Nothing should come *between* you and me, but there may be problems *among* all the candidates.

breath, breathe. *Breath* is the noun, and *breathe* is the verb. Examples: She took a *breath* of fresh air and then continued to *breathe* normally.

can, may. Traditionally, *can* meant "to be able to," and *may* meant "to have permission to." Examples: I *can* send you the report tomorrow. *May* I call to see that it arrived?

capital, capitol. *Capital* refers to the city which is the seat of government and to wealth. *Capitol* means the building where the legislature meets. Examples: We drove to the *capital* and had no trouble find the *Capitol* Building. The plan is to raise *capital* for the highway project.

cite, site, sight. *Cite* means "to refer to." Example: He *cited* several sources. *Site* is a place. Example: The *site* of the new library has been chosen. *Sight* is what our eyes give us. Example: You are a *sight* for sore eyes.

clothes, cloths. People wear *clothes* and use *cloths* to wipe their faces.

coarse, course. *Coarse* is an adjective meaning "rough feeling." Example: Sandpaper is *coarse*. *Course* is a noun that means "a way of going." Example: I took a *course* in speech so that I could follow a new *course* in the company.

compliment, complement. Both are used as nouns and verbs. *Compliment* means "to say something nice," and it also refers to what is said. Examples: He *complimented* her on her good report. She appreciated the *compliment*. *Complement* means "to complete." Examples: The analysis will *complement* the last report. The wine was a nice *complement* to the meal.

conscience, conscious. *Conscience* is having a sense of right and wrong; *conscious* means "being aware." Examples: His *conscience* made him *conscious* of his extreme error in judgment.

contractions. In informal business documents, using contractions, such as *we're*, *you're*, and *it's*, is acceptable. Do not use them in formal reports, proposals, or minutes.

council, counsel. A *council* is a legislative body. *Counsel* as a verb means "to give advice"; as a noun it is the advice itself or an attorney.

decent, descend, dissent. *Decent*, derived from *decency*, means "proper." *Descend* means "to go down." *Dissent* means "to disagree" (verb) or "difference of opinion" (noun).

device, devise. *Device* is the noun meaning "an object used." Example: She took the *device* away from the inept worker. *Devise* [-z sound] is a verb meaning to plan. Example: We *devised* a new strategy to increase sales.

disinterested, uninterested. *Disinterested* means "impartial," whereas *uninterested* means "not interested." Examples: I hope to find a *disinterested*, not an *uninterested*, judge for the contest.

effect, affect. *See affect, effect.*

e.g., i.e. Both are Latin abbreviations for transitions and are followed by a comma. *e.g.* means "for example." Example: We planned several United Way events, *e.g.,* a drawing and a rally. *i.e.* specifies "that is." Example: He will arrive when he can, *i.e.,* at noon.

elicit, illicit. *Elicit* is a verb meaning "to draw out." Example: He tried to *elicit* the information from the suspect. *Illicit* is an adjective meaning "illegal." Example: The *illicit* activity finally came to light.

eminent, imminent. *Eminent* means "outstanding," whereas *imminent* means "occurring very soon." Examples: The arrival of our *eminent* speaker is *imminent*.

except, accept. *See accept, except.*

everyday, every day. *Everyday* is an adjective meaning "ordinary." Example: The *everyday* event had become boring. *Every day* means "each day." Example: We had the boring event *every day*.

farther, further. *Farther* involves distance. Example: He could drive *farther* than anyone in a day. *Further* implies greater amount or degree. Example: She was *further* along with the project than anyone expected.

fewer, less. Like *number* and *amount, fewer* and *less* distinguish countable from indivisible items. Examples: Because our department had *fewer* sales this month [countable], we expect *less* profit [indivisible].

good, well. *Good* is an adjective describing a positive condition. Example: Here is a commendation for your *good* presentation. *Well* is usually an adverb describing how something occurred. Example: You did *well* in your presentation.

immigrate, emigrate. *Immigrate* means "to move into a country," whereas *emigrate* means "to permanently move from one place to another." Examples: The scientist plans to *emigrate* from the Far East and then *immigrate* to the United States.

imply, infer. The speaker *implies*; the listener *infers*. Examples: He *implied* that he would recommend our group. I *inferred* from what he said that he was pleased with our work.

in, into. *In* suggests a location. Example: Put the file *in* the drawer.

Into implies a movement or change. Example: The assistant settled *into* her new position easily.

innocence, innocents. *Innocence* is a condition of blamelessness. *Innocents* are the people who are blameless.

insure, ensure, assure. Traditional usage distinguished between *insure*, meaning "to obtain financial protection," from *ensure*, meaning "to make certain." Current dictionaries now also accept "make certain" as a secondary definition for *insure*. *Assure* means "to promise." Examples: I will *ensure* that he mails the check to *insure* the new car. Can you *assure* me that he has insurance?

its, it's. *Its* is the possessive pronoun. Example: The department always schedules *its* meetings early. *It's* is the contraction meaning "it is." If a pronoun has an apostrophe, it **must** be a contraction (*they're, you're, it's*). No possessive pronoun takes an apostrophe (*his, hers, ours, its*).

lie, lay. *Lie* is an intransitive verb, meaning that it is a complete action in itself and takes no object. Example: I am going to *lie* down. *Lay* is transitive; the action carries through to an object. Example: I will *lay* the report on your desk.

loose, lose. *Loose* is an adjective meaning "not tight." Example: The gem was *loose* in its setting. *Lose* [-z sound] is a verb meaning "to not win or to misplace." Example: The candidate hated to *lose* the election.

may. *See can, may.*

maybe, may be. *Maybe* is an adverb meaning "perhaps." Example: *Maybe* we will go. *May be* is a verb form suggesting a conditional state of being. Example: The report *may be* on her desk.

moral, morale. *Moral* (mōr'-el) is an adjective describing a social judgment. Example: His actions were always *moral*. *Morale* (mo-răl') is a noun that means "mental or emotional condition." Example: Department *morale* was low during the layoffs.

myself. *Myself* is a reflexive or intensive pronoun (like *himself, herself, ourselves*) and requires a double. The doer and the receiver must be the same person. Example: I hit *myself* on the thumb. Do not use it alone. Example [**wrong**]: The client will call George or *myself* when she is ready.

number. *See amount, number.*

passed, past. *Passed* is past tense of *pass*. Example: He *passed* the test. *Past* is a noun or adjective describing former time. Example: In the *past*, we always received our order on time.

patience, patients. *Patience* is a human quality of endurance. *Patients* are sick people.

per. Overly formal business jargon used to replace *pursuant to*, *per* can also mean "according to" or "by means of." Limiting its use to the accurate mathematical usage [fee *per* hour] improves clarity.

percent, percentage. *Percent* (spelled as one word) means one part of a hundred. Example: The election drew only 46 *percent* of eligible voters. *Percentage* means a proportion or share of a total. Example: That *percentage* is terrible.

persecuted, prosecuted. *Persecuted* means "to harass or oppress;" *prosecute* means "to bring to trial." The Israeli government *prosecuted* former Nazi guards who had *persecuted* the inmates.

personnel, personal. *Personnel* (pûr' se-nêl') is a noun meaning "the people in an organization." Example: Our *personnel* are excellent salespersons. *Personal* (pûr' se-nel) is an adjective meaning "private." Example: This is a *personal* message.

phrasal words such as *sign up, shut in, break down,* and *follow up*. These informal words are **usually** spelled as two words when they show action (verbs), hyphenated when they describe (adjectives), and closed up as one word when they name (nouns). Check a current dictionary or style manual to be sure. Examples:

> We will *break down* the display after the show. Here is the *break-down* plan. I almost had a *breakdown*, it was so much work.

> I will *follow up* next week. Do you have the *follow-up* list? [exception] I will call you about your *follow-up*.

precede, proceed. *Precede* means "to go before." Example: I will *precede* you in the processional. Remember that *pre-* means "before." *Proceed* means "to go forward." He will *proceed* to raise the tough questions during the meeting.

principal, principle. *Principal* is "the head of" or "most important." Example: The school *principal* is head of staff. *Principle* is a basic rule. Example: The *principal* reason for my objections rested on our strong *principle* regarding honesty.

quiet, quit, quite. *Quiet* is an adjective meaning "without sound." *Quit* is a verb meaning "to stop." *Quite* is an intensifier meaning "very." Examples: I do not want to *quit* the club because the *quiet* atmosphere is *quite* soothing.

real, really. *Real* is an adjective meaning "authentic." *Really* is an adverb. Examples: We *really* need to work to achieve *real* success.

rise, raise. *Rise* is an intransitive verb, meaning that it is a complete action in itself and takes no object. Example: The sun *rises* in the morning. *Raise* is transitive; the action carries through to an object. Example: I will *raise* the window shade if it's too dark in here.

shall, will. American usage accepts *will* for the future tense of all verbs; *shall* is reserved for formal requests or to show determination. Examples: We *will* go with you to the conference. We *shall* overcome.

sit, set. *Sit* is an intransitive verb, meaning that it is a complete action in itself and takes no object. Example: I am going to *sit* down. *Set* is transitive; the action carries through to an object. Example: I will *set* the report on your desk.

stationary, stationery. *Stationary* is an adjective meaning "unmovable." Example: The *stationary* equipment was rusted. *Stationery* is a noun meaning "paper." I bought new *stationery* for the sales letters.

their, they're, there. *Their* is the possessive pronoun. Example: They asked *their* heir to come visit them. *They're* is a contraction for *they are*. Example: *They're* planning to attend. *There* is an adverb, the opposite of *here*. Example: Put the lamp *there* on the desk.

then, than. *Then* is an adverb identifying time. Example: *Then* they left for the airport. *Than* is a conjunction that involves a comparison. Example: Our competition is more aggressive *than* we are.

thorough, through, though. *Thorough* is an adjective meaning "complete." Example: She performed a *thorough* audit. *Through* is a preposition or adverb meaning "among" or "complete." Examples: When she was *through*, she went *through* all her records. *Though* is a conjunction similar to *although*. Example: We won, even *though* he tripped at the finish line.

to, too, two. *To* is a preposition of direction. Example: I sent the letter *to* the correct address. *Too* means "also." Example: Did you send a letter *too*? *Two* is the number 2.

unique. Meaning one of a kind, *unique* does not take qualifiers. Something is *unique*, **not** very unique.

uninterested, disinterested. *See disinterested, uninterested.*

weather, whether. *Weather* is a noun meaning "climate." *Whether* is a conjunction meaning "if." Examples: We don't know *whether* or not they plan to attend; it depends on the *weather*.

where, were. *Where* is an adverb or conjunction involving place. Example: *Where* do you want to sit? *Were* is the plural past tense form of "to be." Example: We *were* all ready to leave.

who, whom. Use *who* when referring to the actor (subject) or complement. Examples: *Who* called? This is *who*? Use *whom* when referring to the object (receiver of the action). Example: To *whom* do you wish to speak? If in doubt, replace *whom* with *him* to see whether that sounds right.

who, which, that. These are all relative pronouns. *Who* refers to people, and *which* refers to things. Current usage allows using *that* to refer to people or things. Examples: The receptionist *who* answers the phone has a pleasant voice. The product, *which* is new, is selling fast. The group *that* gathered was really upset.

who's, whose. *Who's* is a contraction meaning "who is." Example: *Who's* coming to the meeting? *Whose* is the possessive pronoun. Example: *Whose* turn is it to return the calls?

your, you're. *Your* is the possessive pronoun. Example: *Your* order is ready. *You're* is a contraction meaning *you are*. Example: *You're* at the top of the list.

Careless spelling or inaccurate word choices force readers to translate your meaning. By eliminating this irritation, you also avoid embarrassing errors. *Always* run spellcheck. Then proofread.

Workplace Application

It is a good idea to track words that cause you problems. Put a check in the margin each time you look up a word. Then spend time "reprogramming" your spelling of the word until you no longer have trouble with it. Keep a list of additional word demons in the workspace provided here.

> **"The only stupid thing about words is the spelling of them."**
> —Laura Ingalls Wilder

WORKSPACE

Practice: Word Form

Correct the following sentences for spelling errors and problems of word choice:

1. Part of the chorus went, "How bazaar, how bazaar."

2. He also informed me the "Roscoe" was miss-spelled.

3. If you have any questions in the mean time, please give me a call at 555-4576.

4. The moving of this bed is scaring the walls and the wood doors in the station.

AVOID THE NEW SPEAK OF CYBERSPACE. Emoticons—using icons to express emotion in online text—are not appropriate in workplace writing. Although some, such as the smiley face ☺, are familiar, most are not. Most readers would not recognize the following: :-@ (angry), :-Z (sleeping), or =:-I (punk rocker). The same is true of online chat shorthand: BTW ("by the way") may be common, but DIY ("do it yourself") and AFAYK ("as far as you know") are not. Reader-friendly writers avoid creating translation problems.

Editing

5. For the most part, folk culture depicts rural people in extremely tight-nit family with strong clan ties.

6. Superintendents gave a brief update regarding the statues of the condition of current projects.

7. By finding other economical means to raise revenue in a more efficient way, the governor could better be in position to push his educational reform package.

8. The court accepted the following allegations as true in rending its decision:

9. DOT-regulated machines and horsepowers are effected.

10. People sigh up but fail to show up for the class.

11. At the end of the purge cycle, which lasts 3 minuets, the light will come on.

12. Remove necessary clothing.

Editing

"I think the following rules will cover most cases:

1. Never use a metaphor, simile, or other figure of speech which you are used to seeing in print.

2. Never use a long word where a short one will do.

3. If it is possible to cut a word out, always cut it out.

4. Never use the passive where you can use the active.

5. Never use a foreign word, a scientific word, or a jargon word if you can think of an everyday English equivalent.

6. Break any of these rules sooner than say anything outright barbarous."

—George Orwell
"Politics and the English Language," 1945

Refining

Potential Problems	Strategies
Incorrect and unfocused sentence structure	■ Write complete sentences. ■ Use clear modifiers. ■ Put main idea in sentence core.
Rambling sentences	■ Limit most sentences to one main idea, with modifiers. ■ Do not let sentences run on.
Uninteresting sentences	■ Vary sentence length. ■ Carefully place details. ■ Use parallel structure for series or sentence balance.
Distracting sentence errors	■ Proofread carefully for grammatical correctness, punctuation, and spelling.

Refining

CHAPTER 6—REFINING

Refining

REFINING SENTENCES

What do you notice most? Good writing or poor writing? Most people answer, "Poor—because it is distracting." The irony is that if you write well, readers may not notice. They will be focusing on what you said, not how you said it.

The final step in the writing process involves refining your document to make sure that your readers are not distracted by errors. An analogy helps explain why refining is so critical to your writing success. In the petroleum industry, individuals discover potential hydrocarbon reservoirs [**Planning**], map their production strategy [**Organizing**], drill wells that produce oil and gas [**Writing**], and then transport the raw product through pipelines [**Editing**]. But they cannot sell the product until it is refined. At the refinery, rigorous technical processes take out impurities so that the company can deliver a high-quality product to market.

This chapter presents what you need to know about removing the impurities from your written product. It outlines the most common errors in sentence structure, word formation, punctuation, and mechanics. Chapter 8, "Fundamentals," includes a brief overview of the basic designs of English grammar. For answers to more complex or unusual questions about grammar and mechanics, you should consult a good reference manual.

At this **Refining**—or quality control—stage of the writing process, you should revise your written product for clarity and correctness in the following:

Sentence Structure

- Fragments
- Comma splices or fused sentences
- Run-on sentences
- Dangling modifiers
- Parallel structure

Word Formation

- Verb forms
- Subject-verb agreement
- Pronoun usage
- Spelling

Punctuation

- End punctuation
- Commas
- Colons
- Semicolons
- Apostrophes
- Hyphens
- Quotation marks

Mechanics

- Numbers
- Dates
- Abbreviations
- Capitalization

> **"Many factors influence the distinction between reading that is easy and reading that is hard. Unfamiliar words will cause a stumble. The sentence that is needlessly long will steal our attention. Strange foreign phrases, obscure allusions, inapt quotations, patent errors in grammar or spelling—all these are enemies to pleasant comprehension."**
>
> —James J. Kilpatrick

Self-Assessment: Grammar and Punctuation

Many people worry about their grammar—the "G" word. To determine how well you catch errors, correct the following memo. Then compare your changes to the corrected version at the end of the chapter so that you are aware of errors you may be missing in your own documents. You will find answers to all the practice exercises in Chapter 7, "Practice."

Judy Smith and myself was discussing the suspension of employees when they take an in service withdrawal of the Investment Plus or Thrift Plan. Judy would like to know what procedures for the group is in place for Tom Johnson and/or the payroll department, etc. to start and stop a suspension.

I recently sent a memo to Susan Thompson regarding a employee currently suspended in the thrift plan so that their suspension would not be interrupt do to the changes in the Plan, I've attached a copy of the memo sent to Susan for you information.

Also do we continue to in put the "Thrift Plan Date" on Benefit's screen 3 when employee initially joins the plan. And if we are to continue. How do we know when an employee joins the Plan so we can input this date in to the program?

Thanks for your help in this matters.

WORKSPACE

CONTROLLING SENTENCES

We do not make meaning in English simply with words. We make meaning with sentences—words used in a certain order, based on formulas we imprinted in our language computers when we learned to speak. Chapter 8, "Fundamentals," contains a very basic outline of these grammar formulas for forming sentences and words. We use these formulas to control sentence correctness and to write more interesting and effective sentences. Here are some guidelines.

Correct Major Sentence Errors

Sentences consist of one or more clauses. A clause is a group of words that includes a subject (who or what?) and a predicate (verb—what action?). An *independent* clause (or sentence) can stand alone because it expresses a complete thought. A *dependent* clause must be connected to a sentence. Several common sentence errors result from misusing clauses.

Write complete sentences, not fragments.

Sentence fragments do not express a complete thought, even though they may include a subject and a verb. Adding an introductory word such as *because, if, since, that,* or *who* makes a clause dependent, or no longer a complete thought. In other fragments, the verb phrase is incomplete.

Independent Clause:	He sent me the report.

Dependent Clauses:	*Because* he sent me the report. *If* he sent me the report. *Although* he sent me the report. ... *that* he sent me the report. ... *who* sent me the report.	**Subordinating conjunctions** such as *because, when, if,* and *although* create adverbial dependent clauses. **Relative pronouns** such as *that, who,* and *which* create adjective dependent clauses.
Verb Phrases:	The manager *having sent* me the report. The manager *to complete* the report.	Verbal phrases (participles and infinitives) act as modifiers and cannot stand alone.

To correct sentence fragments, connect the incomplete phrase or clause to a complete clause. Or change the word or phrase so that the sentence can stand alone:

Fragment:	*Because* he sent me the report.
Correct:	*Because* he sent me the report, I could finish the project.
Fragment:	The manager *having sent* me the report.
Correct:	The manager *had sent* me the report.

Practice: Fragments

Correct the following sentence fragments:

1. After she left my office. I found the file she had been looking for.

2. Per your telephone conversation with Susan Smith about your above mentioned account.

3. The error having been corrected.

4. Acknowledging receipt of your letter dated May 14, 200_.

5. They will listen to a problem and hear you out, before trouble shooting. Great qualities for any team.

Correct the punctuation in comma splices and fused sentences.

In sentences that have two or more independent clauses, you can punctuate the independent clauses in three ways. The last two form **compound sentences**.

1. With a **period to form separate sentences:**

He sent me a report. However, it was incomplete.

2. With a **comma and coordinating conjunction:**
[*and, or, but, so, yet, for*]

He sent me a report, **but** *it was incomplete.*

3. With a **semicolon:**
[Transitional words such as *therefore* and *then* can be used with this option, but are not required.]

He sent me a report; **however**, *it was incomplete.*

Using a comma or no punctuation between full sentences creates errors called the comma splice or fused sentence:

Comma Splice: *He sent me a report, however, it was incomplete.*

Fused Sentence: *He sent me a report however, it was incomplete.*

Correct: *He sent me a report. However, it was incomplete.*
     He sent me a report; however, it was incomplete.

These sentence errors confuse readers because they do not clearly separate equally important ideas.

Rules of the Sentence Punctuation Road

- **A period is a stop sign.**

- **A comma is a yield sign.**

- **A semicolon is a rolling stop —legal in grammar!**

Refining

Do not confuse the semicolon with the colon.

These punctuation marks show very different relationships within the sentence:

- The semicolon, like the fulcrum on a seesaw, balances two complete sentences with *equal*, closely related ideas.

  We have undergone some major changes in our area; therefore, I need to monitor this desk more closely during the transition.

- The colon, like a dam, separates an abstract concept in a complete sentence from the specific details that explain it. It reveals an *unequal* relationship.

  We have undergone some major changes in our area: reducing staff, adjusting responsibilities, and eliminating all travel and entertainment expenses.

Practice: Sentence Errors

Correct the following sentences:

1. They shipped more than we ordered, I don't know why they would issue a credit.

2. I hope to receive your answer next week if not I'll call you then we can discuss the project.

3. In addition to a major commitment in terms of personnel, space, telephone lines and equipment; managing an on-going telemarketing sales effort requires skill and dedication.

4. I would like two sets of pictures of your establishment. One for my files and one to send in to an architectural magazine.

5. The elevator is not running again—it must need a new electrical system.

Refining

Focus your meaning on the core sentence elements—the subject and verb—to avoid awkward sentences.

The simplest sentences have only a subject and verb plus possibly an object or complement:

> *She ran.*
> *George bought a car.*
> *He is a good worker.*

This primer style is correct but boring. As we mature as writers, we learn to add modifiers to sentences, thus adding details and more interesting rhythms:

> *She ran away from the very large, teeth-baring dog.*
>
> *Because he could not stand another long walk to work, George bought a car.*
>
> *In spite of rumors that he landed the job with his family connections, he handles all tasks well except typing.*

Identifying the subject-verb is helpful not because you need to know grammatical terms to write sentences. You do not. But it does help you focus awkward sentences. Often you can untangle a sentence by finding the subject and verb, then asking, "Is that my central idea?" You may also ask, "Is that a complete sentence?" If not, think about what you *are* trying to say. Then focus your point in the sentence core.

See Chapter 8 for a summary of sentence core elements.

Vary your sentence structure.

Recognizing the core elements also helps you add variety to your sentences. If every sentence begins with subject-verb, the effect is boring. Just as sentences should vary in length, so too they should avoid a repetitious structure. Notice that in this and the previous section, the sentences vary in length, in complexity, in opening elements, in core elements, and in use of parallel structure.

A good rule of thumb is that sentences should average no more than 21 words. That means you will have long sentences, but they will be offset by short ones. Put really important points in short sentences—for emphasis.

Refining

Combine short, choppy sentences.

To avoid sentences that sound like a first-grade primer, combine ideas to modify one main point. The exception is if you have two or more equally important ideas you want to balance. Then you would use a compound sentence.

Primer Style: *Mark the check void. Then put a note on the check as to the reason that we have voided the check out. (It was a duplicate payment.) Send the check to Tom Smith, 154 S. Main, mc e111, Center City, OK 74103. Or send it to me. It will be backed off the account.*

Revised: *Mark the check void, and then put a note on the check about why we have voided it out (duplicate payment). Send the check to Tom Smith, 154 S. Main, mc e111, Center City, OK 74103 or to me. It will be backed off the account.*

Break up run-on sentences.

Run-on, or overcombined, sentences present too many ideas for the reader to remember. These need to be divided into shorter units or tightened by making some ideas modifiers.

Run-on: *The operator I spoke with was Shirley and after giving her all the background information she told me it would be perfectly okay to do this and would make all the necessary changes on the computer.*

Revised: *I spoke with the operator Shirley. After I explained all the background information, she said doing this would be perfectly okay. She would make all the necessary changes in the computer.*

Practice: Sentence Focus

Revise these sentences to focus ideas more clearly:

1. According to our station attendant on duty at the time of the accident, Mr. Jones saw a girl that he knew and sped away from the pumps in great haste in order to catch up with her and was certainly not paying attention to safe driving when he collided with the very obvious utility pole.

2. Our board room has an SL-1 phone and should not be unplugged.

3. If so, are the calculations the same, and in addition to the reports enclosed, what additional reports are necessary to assist management in controlling inventories?

4. Go into the control panel and click the "modem Icon" and view which manufacturer of your modem and then return to "Msmail" under the connect menu and select "Communications" and then pick a script that has the name similar to your modem manufacturer and click ok and try again.

Connect dangling and misplaced modifiers to the words they modify.

Recognizing dangling or misplaced modifiers can be tricky. A descriptive modifier must connect to the word it modifies. If the word is implied or buried elsewhere in the sentence, the modifier will dangle, possibly confusing or amusing the reader. Example: *Having rotted in the basement, my brother carried the potatoes to the kitchen.*

Dangling: *Therefore, I respectfully request that you forward me at your earliest convenience the materials for that course. **If not available**, a refund of the $150 is appreciated.* [Was the refund not available?]

Correct: *Therefore, please send me the materials for the course at your earliest convenience. If **they are** not available, please refund the $150.*

Dangling: *By closing our books* at the end of the calendar year, our tax accounting was simplified.
[Who closed the books?]

Correct: *Because we closed our books* at the end of the calendar year, our tax accounting was simplified.

Correct: *Closing our books at the end of the year simplified our tax accounting.*

Misplaced: *The employee was wiping off the end of a pipe that had fallen into the mud **with his gloved hand**.*
[Is his hand lying in the mud?]

Correct: *With **his gloved hand**, the employee was wiping off the end of a pipe that had fallen into the mud.*

Practice: Dangling Modifiers

Revise these sentences so that the modifiers are connected clearly to the words they modify and the sentences are punctuated correctly:

1. Central Technology's Year End is June 30, 200_, ALL CLASSES prior to this date must be turned in before June 29, 200_, to be eligible for assistance.

2. Hoping to improve the group's safety record, the training sessions were scheduled for five consecutive weeks.

3. Recently, the Sales Representative for my accounts promised my client that the operations team could and would perform a manual process without receiving approval from the Operations Manager.

4. To begin operations immediately, the materials must be in the warehouse by Monday.

Create parallel structure for items in a series or in balance.

Parallel structure occurs when several words, phrases, or clauses are deliberately arranged in a similar structure to support similar content. Strong parallel structure creates clarity and emphasis:

■ The new debenture provided cash *to expand the current assets* and *to retire short-term debt*.
  [*repeated verbal phrases*]

■ Typically the drugs are ones that the larger pharmaceutical companies do not want to make *because the market is too small, the delivery media is uncommon, or some other complicating matter makes them unattractive*.
  [*series of dependent clauses*]

■ Data Systems and Processing will:

  1. *Perform* a technical review and, if required, *ensure* that the proposed hardware and/or software is compatible with existing systems.

  2. *Review* the required economic justification.

  3. *Work* with the appropriate corporate department to obtain the required approvals.
     [*series based on action verbs*]

Parallelism creates correctness and readability problems if:

■ A series presents similar ideas in different structures:

  Faulty: Implementing vendor-specific validations will:
  a) **Decrease** error/rejection rates.
  b) **Necessitating** fewer supplements and less provisioning/vendor communications.
  c) **Decrease** both order cost and order time.
  d) **This will allow us** greater applicability of our forms since our agreements are only valid for clean (error-free) orders.

  Correct: Implementing vendor-specific validations will:
  a) **Decrease** error/rejection rates.
  b) **Necessitate** fewer supplements and less provisioning/vendor communication.
  c) **Decrease** both order cost and order time.
  d) **Create** greater applicability of our forms since our agreements are only valid for clean (error-free) orders.

■ Items in a balanced construction do not match.

Faulty: You have helped thousands of people **not only enjoy their experience** at the zoo, **but also have influenced** how they view wild animals and their relationship to man.

Correct: You **not only have helped thousands** of people enjoy their experience at the zoo, **but also have influenced** how they view wild animals and their relationship to man.
[*compound verbs telling what "you" have done*]

Practice: Parallelism

Complete the series in each of the following sentences, using parallel structure:

1. The current changes are proposed to facilitate the departmental filing system and _____ more detailed address information.

2. This decision was based on low cost, instant availability, and _____.

3. My accomplishments last quarter:

    a. Created more efficient accounting form;

    b. Conducted and _____ two important negotiations;

    c. _____ your duties when you were on other assignments;

    d. _____ an urgent correspondence letter-routing system.

Practice: Sentence Errors

Correct the following sentences for run-on sentences, fragments, comma splices/fused sentences, dangling modifiers, and parallel structure:

1. I will retain copies of your requests and should these people desire to schedule a class in January, I will place them at the top of the list.

2. Our concerns are many, but heading the list is possible equipment damage and if something does happen to our #3 pump it is conceivable that we simply would not be able to bring on another pump, unless we could convince the electric company to crank up the voltage.

3. Hoping this will handle the problem.

4. This is a rush, the report is due soon.

5. In an effort to track the number of training hours the staff receives, I would appreciate a quarterly report from you listing employee name, course, and/or seminar completed. Also the number of training hours for your direct reports.

6. I'm sorry it wasn't with the rest of the papers, I checked with our Auditor's office and they were not holding it for any reason.

7. Not everyone has a first hand personal knowledge of the dedicated staff you have, we see them everyday, and do appreciate your services.

8. By properly parking along one side of the alley adequate space would be available for one way traffic through the alley.

9. If approved, Mrs. Smith requests two copies be returned to her office.

10. I really like your staff; they have a great attitude, very friendly, and willing to help.

11. However, the three principals decided that retention of heifers would allow for better quality of milk, command higher milk prices due to that quality, and with lower costs.

Practice: Correcting Sentences

Correct all sentence errors in the following passage:

The bank where the fiber was damaged was allegedly located; and marked with orange paint by the technician. There was no apparent marking of a flag. Railway called for an identification on March 15, 200_, copies of one-call record placed by ATR are available. Another technician and the line supervisor could not verify that the area was marked by paint, and Railroad claimed there was no marking, so there is a major problem of non verification about the accuracy of the initial report. According to the technician, that allegedly marked the area, there was rain in the area three days prior to the Railroad drilling and the rain apparently washed the paint marks off of the area, leaving no sign and without proof.

Beware the grammar checker on your computer! It can mislead you into thinking something is wrong (like a passive verb or a comma before every "which"). It can also miss errors (such as "it's" vs. "its").

The grammar and spelling checkers are only aids—not substitutes for proofreading.

Refining

CONTROLLING WORD FORMS

Grammar errors are often mistakes in word formation. For example, a missing –s can create a subject-verb agreement error. A dropped –ed makes a verb present tense when it should be past tense. Some errors result from the nonstandard word forms we heard when we were learning to speak. These dialect errors hurt our credibility. Chapter 8 includes an overview of how we form words, with special emphasis on correct verb forms. This section addresses the common errors that make us look careless and unprofessional.

Use Verbs Correctly

Native speakers of a language are usually unaware of all the rules of verb formation because they acquired the formulas as children. If you do have problems with verbs, remember these tips for consistent and correct usage:

Maintain the same tense in a narrative. Going from past to present to past is distracting for readers.

Incorrect:	*Mr. Johnson **explained** he had been involved in a vehicle accident and the other driver had left the scene of the accident. Mr. Johnson **goes** on to explain he followed the other driver to a location and **was** now located in front of a house but **is** not sure where he was.*
Correct:	*Mr. Johnson **explained** he had been involved in a vehicle accident and the other driver had left the scene of the accident. Mr. Johnson **went** on to explain he followed the other driver to a location, **was** now located in front of a house, but he **was** not sure where.* [all past tense]

Choose the simplest form of the verb if you are not implying a special meaning. Simple past can often replace a perfect form.

*We **went** to town* instead of *We **had gone** to town.*

Use auxiliaries such as "must," "should," or "could" to replace wordy phrases.

For example, *We **must go*** can replace *It is imperative that we go.*

Use the standard forms of verbs to avoid dialect errors.

Incorrect: *We **was intending** to complete the project this week.*

Correct: *We **were intending** to complete the project this week.
[plural subject and verb]*

Incorrect: *The officer **begun to** speak.*

Correct: *The officer **began to** speak. [past tense]*

Correct: *The officer **had begun** to speak.
[have + the past participle]*

Regular Verbs

Regular verbs follow consistent formation patterns, using the same endings for the different forms of the verb:

Form	Ending	Example
present tense	none = base form	look
3rd person singular, present tense	+ -*s*	looks
present participle	+ -*ing*	looking
past tense	+ -*ed*	looked
past participle	+ -*ed*	looked

Irregular Verbs

Irregular verbs take many forms. The simple past tense and the past participle, instead of both ending in -*ed*, are different. Also, while the -*en* ending is common in the past participle, it is not universal. To avoid embarrassing dialect errors, you must memorize the correct forms.

Wrong: *We **seen** him at the cafeteria.*

Right: *We **saw** him at the cafeteria. [simple past tense]*

    *We **had seen** him at the cafeteria every day this week.
[past perfect tense]*

Wrong: *The program **had ran** overnight.*

Right: *The program **ran** overnight. [simple past tense]*

    *The program **had run** overnight. [past perfect tense]*

Dictionaries show only the base form for regular verbs but all forms for irregular verbs. Table 6-1 outlines the different forms for common irregular verbs. Refer to Chapter 8 for more detail about the principal parts of verbs and the formula for creating different verb tenses and modes.

Table 6-1. Irregular Verb Forms

Base Form	Present Tense (3rd sing.)	Past Tense	Past Participle	Present Participle
be	am, is, are	was, were	been	being
become	-s	became	become	becoming
begin	-s	began	begun	beginning
blow	-s	blew	blown	blowing
break	-s	broke	broken	breaking
bring	-s	brought	brought	bringing
build	-s	built	built	building
buy	-s	bought	bought	buying
catch	catches	caught	caught	catching
choose	chooses	chose	chosen	choosing
come	-s	came	come	coming
cost	-s	cost	cost	costing
do	does	did	done	doing
drag	-s	dragged	dragged	dragging
draw	-s	drew	drawn	drawing
drink	-s	drank	drunk	drinking
drive	-s	drove	driven	driving
eat	-s	ate	eaten	eating
fall	-s	fell	fallen	falling
feel	-s	felt	felt	feeling
find	-s	found	found	finding
fly	flies	flew	flown	flying
forget	-s	forgot	forgotten, forgot	forgetting
get	-s	got	gotten, got	getting
give	-s	gave	given	giving
go	goes	went	gone	going
grow	-s	grew	grown	growing
have	has	had	had	having
hear	-s	heard	heard	hearing
hide	-s	hid	hidden	hiding
hit	-s	hit	hit	hitting
hold	-s	held	held	holding
keep	-s	kept	kept	keeping
know	-s	knew	known	knowing
lay ["*to place*" *transitive*]	-s	laid	laid	laying
lead	-s	led	led	leading
lie ["*recline*" *intransitive*]	-s	lay	lain	lying
lose	-s	lost	lost	losing

(continued)

Table 6-1. Irregular Verb Forms *(concluded)*

Base Form	Present Tense (3rd sing.)	Past Tense	Past Participle	Present Participle
make	-s	made	made	making
pay	-s	paid	paid	paying
prove	-s	proved	proven	proving
read [rēd]	-s	read [rĕd]	read [rĕd]	reading
ride	-s	rode	ridden	riding
rise	-s	rose	risen	rising
run	-s	ran	run	running
say	-s	said	said	saying
see	-s	saw	seen	seeing
sell	-s	sold	sold	selling
send	-s	sent	sent	sending
set ["*place*" transitive]	-s	set	set	setting
sing	-s	sang	sung	singing
sit [*intransitive*]	-s	sat	sat	sitting
sleep	-s	slept	slept	sleeping
speak	-s	spoke	spoken	speaking
stand	-s	stood	stood	standing
strike	-s	struck	struck, stricken	stiking
swear	-s	swore	sworn	swearing
take	-s	took	taken	taking
teach	teaches	taught	taught	teaching
tell	-s	told	told	telling
think	-s	thought	thought	thinking
throw	-s	threw	thrown	throwing
understand	-s	understood	understood	understanding
wear	-s	wore	worn	wearing
write	-s	wrote	written	writing

Active versus Passive Voice

Prefer active to passive verbs. Even though grammar checkers highlight passive verbs—as if they are wrong—they are perfectly correct grammatically. However, using too many passive verbs adds unnecessary words and robs your sentences of the energy derived from "Who or what does what to whom" (active voice). Refer to Chapter 5 for practice in transforming passive voice to active voice.

With verbs in the passive voice, the **subject** (S) of the sentence **receives** the action of the verb (V), and the actor is in an actual or implied "by" prepositional phrase (see Table 6-2).

Table 6-2. Passive Voice vs. Active Voice

Subject	Passive Voice S-V		Active Voice S-V-O
	Form of *to be* as the auxiliary	**Main verb in past participle form**	
Susan	**is** *(present tense)*	**admired** *by all.*	*All admire Susan.*
The report	**was** *(past tense)*	**written** *in Spanish.*	*He wrote the report in Spanish.*
The test	**will be** *(future tense)*	**given** *today.*	*I will give the test today.*

Create Subject-Verb Agreement

In English, the subject (S) of a sentence must agree with the verb (V) in number. If the subject is plural, the verb must be too. This rule seems easy enough to observe, but other structures in English complicate the issue.

■ Plural nouns end in "*s*," but singular verbs in the present tense also end in "*s*." This apparent contradiction can be confusing.

> The **girls** *love ice cream.*
> The girl **loves** *ice cream.*

■ The subject and verb are often separated by words or clauses that explain the subject:

> Subject   [+ modifiers]   +Verb
> *The accountant [in the front office] called.*

Sometimes nouns closer to the verb seem to be the subject. It is easy to make the verb agree with the nearest noun instead of the real subject.

> **Incorrect:**   *The **list** of reports **are enclosed**.*
> **Correct:**   *The **list** of reports **is enclosed**.*

■ By definition, some pronouns are singular (*each, everyone, everybody*), whereas others are plural (*all, both, some*). "*None*" can be singular or plural, depending on the context.

> **Each** *of them* **is planning** *to play a part.*
> **All** *of them* **are planning** *to play a part.*

> **None** *of the shipment* **is** *in the warehouse.*
> **None** *of us* **are planning** *to attend.*
> **Everyone is planning** *to go.*

> "Good grammar, I suggest, equates with good manners. Try not to belch at the table, darling, and do remember that a singular subject demands a singular verb. For good or ill, we are betrayed by our speech."
> —James J. Kilpatrick

Refining

■ Sometimes the subject and verb are reversed. Because the first word (in the normal subject slot) does not end in "*s*," it is easy to assume that the verb should be singular.

> There *are* several **suggestions** to consider.
>   *V*   *S*

> **Enclosed are** the **reports** you requested.
>   *V*   *S*

> **Attached** is the **invoice** you are expecting.
>   *V*   *S*

■ Compound subjects with "*and*" always take a plural verb. If neither subject ends in "*s*," it is easy to assume the verb should be singular.

> The **report** on our status and the **list are** correct.
>   *S*   *S* *V*

■ For compound subjects with "*or*" or "*nor*," the verb agrees with the subject closest to it.

>   *S*   *S*   *V*
> Either the **report** on our status or the **lists** of attendees **are** incorrect.

>   *S*   *S*   *V*
> Neither the **lists** of attendees nor the **report** on our status **is** correct.

■ Subjects consisting of phrases or dependent clauses always take singular verbs.

> <u>Running a large company</u> **is** a complex task.
>   *S*   *V*

> <u>How we will build a consensus</u> **is** the main agenda item.
>   *S*   *V*

■ The verb in a dependent adjective clause agrees with the noun that "*who*," "*whom*," "*which*," or "*that*" refers to.

>   *S*   *adjective clause*   *V*
> The **woman** <u>who is training our staff</u> **likes** to have music playing in the room.

Some examples:

Incorrect:	*Once again, your **time and consideration is** appreciated.*
Correct:	*Once again, your **time and consideration are** appreciated.*
Incorrect:	*The process halts when **one** of a set of user-defined conditions **are met**.*
Correct:	*The process halts when **one** of a set of user-defined conditions **is met**.*
Incorrect:	*The **manner** in which the loans are processed **are** as follows.*
Correct:	*The **manner** in which the loans are processed **is** as follows.*
Correct:	*The **loans are processed** as follows.*
Incorrect:	*There **is** no available **employees** that can perform these tasks.*
Correct:	*There **are** no available **employees** that can perform these tasks.*
Correct:	*No **employees are** available who can perform these tasks.*

Practice: Subject-Verb Agreement

Correct the subject-verb agreement errors in the following sentences:

1. On July 2, 200_, a notification letter requesting receipts for this month were sent to you.

2. As sonar technology and laser technology is implemented, additional OT or IT positions will have to be reclassified.

Refining

3. Completing the forms do not obligate you to become a volunteer.

4. However, assuming any motions are allowable, each are defeated.

5. Neither Johnson, nor Peterson, were principals, officers, directors, shareholders, or managers of the company.

6. If there is any further questions that I can answer for you please contact me at ext. 1234.

7. The alarm status of the switches are updated as status changes.

Use Pronouns Correctly

By definition, a *pro*noun takes the place of a noun. Therefore, to clearly connect ideas, a pronoun follows a noun, clearly refers to it, and agrees with the noun in number.

Make a pronoun agree in number with the noun it replaces.
Noun/pronoun agreement makes our sentences "add up."

Incorrect:	Send the **employee** form to *their* attention.
Correct:	Send the **employees'** forms to *their* attention.
Correct:	Send the form to the employee.

People disagree about how to handle generic, singular nouns such as "employee." Using the masculine *he* or *him* to refer to all humans is out of date. But so far there is no agreement about an acceptable alternative, such as *they* or the clumsy *he/she*. Your best choices are to make both the noun or pronoun plural if you can, or avoid the issue by using *"a"* or *"the"*—for example, *Send the employee a form.*

Use singular pronouns to refer to collective nouns, such as *"group"* or *"committee"* unless a plural meaning is implied.

Incorrect: *The **committee** is planning to sponsor **their** golf outing.*

Correct: *The **committee** is planning to sponsor **its** golf outing.*
*The **committee** is planning to sponsor **a** golf outing.*
*The **committee** all stood to accept **their** plaques.*

Use the correct number to refer to indefinite pronouns that are singular (*each, everyone, everybody*) or plural (*all, both, some*). Or avoid using a pronoun.

*__Each__ of them is planning to play **his** or **her** part.*
*__All__ of them are planning to play **their** parts.*
*__All__ of them are planning to play **a** part.*

*__Everyone__ is going to wear **his or her** coat.*
*__Everyone__ is going to wear **a** coat.*

Make demonstrative pronouns (*this, that, these,* and *those*) clearly refer to a noun and agree with the noun in number.

Incorrect: The agent offered several ***policy options. This*** constituted his portfolio.

Correct: The agent offered several ***policy options. These*** constituted his portfolio.

Check for pronouns that do not clearly refer to nouns. The pronouns *this, which,* and *it* are often used carelessly to refer to the entire preceding idea rather than to a particular noun. You can easily correct this broad reference and improve clarity by inserting a noun after *this* or before *which*. Replace *it* with a noun.

Vague: We will begin the project by meeting next week. ***This*** will enable us to address important questions promptly.

Clearer: We will begin the project by meeting next week. ***This schedule*** will enable us to address important questions promptly.

Vague: The meeting lasted until 6:00 p.m., *which* made me late for dinner.

Clearer: The meeting lasted until 6:00 p.m., *a delay which* made me late for dinner.

Vague: To get *it* off the ground, we need to assign responsibilities.

Clearer: To get *the project* off the ground, we need to assign responsibilities.

Use personal pronouns in the correct case, or form. The case is determined by the pronoun's function in the sentence, as shown in Table 6-3.

Table 6-3. Cases of Personal and Relative Pronouns

Personal Pronouns			
Person	**As Subjects and Complements**	**As Objects**	**As Possessives**
Singular 1	I	me	my, mine
2	you	you	your, yours
3	he	him	his
	she	her	her, hers
	it	it	its
Plural 1	we	us	our, ours
2	you	you	your, yours
3	they	them	their, theirs
Relative Pronouns			
	who whoever	whom whomever	whose whosever
Note:		Notice that -*m* ends several objective pronouns—*him* is like *whom*.	Notice that -*s* ends several possessive pronouns. No possessive pronoun has an apostrophe, even *its*.

Incorrect:	May I speak to Joan? This is *her*.
Correct:	May I speak to Joan? This is *she*. [complement]

Correct:	If you plan to attend, give *me* a call. [indirect object]
Correct:	If you plan to attend, send the card to *me*. [object of the preposition]

Incorrect:	He had more influence than *me*.
Correct:	He had more influence than *I* [had]. [subject]

Incorrect:	*Him and me* are planning to win the tournament.
Correct:	*He and I* are planning to win the tournament. [subjects]

Who and Whom. *Who* and *whom* have the same cases as *he* and *him*. Try substituting those words as the answer to the question to see what sounds right.

> To *whom* do you wish to speak? I want to speak to *him*.
> *Who* called? *He* called.

Use *who* and *whom* to refer to *people* and *which* to refers to things. *That* may refer to both people and things.

Use the correct case in compound constructions, and put yourself last. To check, drop one part of the compound. If the remaining pronoun does not sound right alone, it probably is not.

Incorrect:	He sent the report to Tom and *I*. *He sent the report to I?*
	He sent the report to Tom and *myself*. *He sent the report to myself?*
	He sent the report to *me* and Tom.
Correct:	He sent the report to Tom and *me*.

Use the possessive pronoun form with gerunds (verbs ending in *-ing* and functioning like a noun).

Incorrect:	The committee members resented *him* talking to the press without their approval.
Correct:	The committee members resented *his* talking to the press without their approval.

Use the *-self* pronouns only if there is a doubling in the sentence. These pronouns are correct only when the doer and the receiver refer to the same person or thing (**reflexive**) or when the person's involvement is emphasized (**intensive**).

Reflexive:	*George* gave *himself* a raise.
Intensive:	*Susan* completed the report all by *herself*.

Many people, trying to avoid the *he/him* or *I/me* issue, incorrectly choose a *-self* pronoun:

Wrong:	Send the bill to Janet or *myself*.
Right:	Send the bill to Janet or *me*.
Wrong:	I signed *me* up for the course.
Right:	I signed *myself* up for the course.
Wrong:	*Myself and Gary* were up for a raise.
Right:	*Gary and I* were up for a raise.

Practice: Pronouns

Correct the following sentences for pronoun errors:

1. Within a few minutes she responded to my e-mail and submitted Pam a list. She is supposed to be working on that list today.

2. Susan and her agreed to accept responsibility for the United Way drive.

3. Jim and I both agree that Larry, Jim, and myself should outline another approach to developing this business.

4. Each band will perform their own style of music.

5. Our facilities are unique in that most are built in neighborhoods. This enables individuals, especially senior citizens and youth who are not mobile, easy access to quality social, fitness, and sports opportunities.

6. It would be appreciated if the contract could be prepared as soon as possible for consideration. This would be very helpful in that, it will be more cost effective to integrate the proposed project with other remodeling projects currently in progress.

Check Your Spelling

Everyone has occasional problems with spelling. Often errors come from carelessness, from not taking the time to review what has been written. Some people do not see that the letters have been reversed or omitted. Other spelling errors result from laziness, from not looking up questionable spelling in a dictionary and then memorizing the correct form. In every case, lack of proofreading is the major cause.

Spelling errors would be forgivable if they did not immediately create such a bad impression. Even the best memo—or even e-mail—appears inaccurate or illiterate if it is sprinkled with misspelled words. It shouts to the reader, "My writer did not bother with quality control."

Some general suggestions and specific spelling rules may help you avoid creating such a negative impression.

Learn to spell the words you use regularly. Do not allow bad habits to develop in spelling the special vocabulary of your profession or commonly used words.

Buy and use a small dictionary or administrative assistant's spelling guide. When you check on a word's spelling, mark the word in the guide to remind yourself that you needed help. When a word collects several marks, memorize it.

Remember some basic word formation rules:

- Plural nouns and acronyms usually end in *-s.* (girl*s*, SST*s*)

- When a noun ends in *-s, -x, -ch, -sh,* or *-z,* add *-es* to form the plural. (wish*es*, church*es*)

- To form a plural when a noun ends in a consonant + *-y,* change the *-y* to *-i* and add *-es.* (cop*y*, cop*ies*)

- Singular nouns that show possession end in *-'s.* (girl*'s*, woman*'s*)

- For plural possessive nouns, form the plural first and then add *'* or *-'s.* (girl*s'*, women*'s*)

- Verbs in the past tense often end in *-ed.* (ask*ed*)

- *Double the final consonant* when adding a suffix starting with a vowel to a word ending in a single vowel + a single consonant. (hit/hit*ting*, swim/swim*mer*)

- Words ending in silent *-e* usually drop the *-e* before a suffix beginning with a vowel. (arriv*e*/arriv*al*, argu*e*/ argu*ing*)

Always run spellcheck. Then proofread carefully. Do not skim over words without seeing them. Read them outloud. Read backwards, one word at a time. In other words, be concerned about correct spelling.

Practice: Word Formation

Correct the following sentences, paying particular attention to errors in word formation—spelling, verb forms, subject-verb agreement, and pronoun usage:

1. But as the years have gone by, inflation and other factors has raised the cost of living.

2. Mr. Johnson explained he had been involved in a vehicle accident and the other driver had left the scene of the accident. Mr. Johnson goes on to explain he followed the other driver to a location and was now located in front of a house but is not sure where he was.

3. John told you, Carman Simpson, and myself, he had been on our location at the original meeting.

4. Circles on the tabulation indicates low bids.

5. Each suspect stated they received payment for passing the counterfeited checks.

6. Either I or Ron will let you know the results of the review and what our recommendation is.

7. Financial support, like volunteer workers and effective speakers, are hard to get.

8. Then each month your customer pays their bill, you will receive a monthly residual of up to $3 for the lifetime of the customers' subscription.

9. If a company fails to properly market their high tech products they will often fail to meet their potential in the marketplace.

10. If there are less than five companies who post the type of crude then they are averaged.

11. Each of these subpoenas address separate categories of requested documents.

12. It would be appreciated if the contract could be prepared as soon as possible for consideration. This would be very helpful in that, it will be more cost effective to integrate the proposed project with other remodeling projects currently in progress.

Practice: Proofreading for Word Errors

Correct all errors in the memo in the following memo:

To:	Jim Smith
From:	Larry Johnson
Date:	Jan. 3, 200_
Subject:	New Vacation Schedule

Because every one in the Department try to take vacations at Christmas time, we are left understaffed at a busy time of the year. This effects the efficiency of the department and makes it impossible to close the books before the end of the year report.

Next year there are a requirement that every employee should request vacation by their seniorty with only 5 allowed to vacation at Christmas. By seperating vacation times we can avoid the understaffing problem and still allows alot of flexibility in scheduling.

WORKSPACE

Practice: Proofreading

Correct all sentence and word formation errors in the following memo:

> Every motor carrier according to the regulators have to establish a Employee Assistance Program (EAP) for their drivers and supervisor to use.
>
> The EAP is suppose to consist of training programs for the supervisory personal and all drivers. It should include the affects and consequences of using illegal drugs and alcohol in regards to personal health, safety, and the work environment. The program also covers changes that indicates abuse and documentation of training given to the supervisory personal and drivers'.
>
> If you now of an employee which needs help, have them call the following hot line number: 800-555-5151.

WORKSPACE

Figure 6-1 is a quick reference to the grammatical structures that require punctuation. Though it is not an exhaustive model, it does cover almost all the punctuation you will use in your ordinary writing tasks. If a construction is not listed, you probably do not need punctuation, or it is such an odd usage that even experts have to look it up. Use these Quick Tips as your first reference for punctuation questions. Brackets [ ] mean that an element is optional.

PUNCTUATION COUNTS!

An English professor wrote the words "woman without her man is nothing" on the board and told the students to punctuate it correctly.

The men wrote: "Woman, without her man, is nothing."

The women wrote: "Woman! Without her, man is nothing."

Refining

QUICK TIPS ON PUNCTUATION

BETWEEN FULL SENTENCES	Sentence. Sentence.
	Sentence, and/or/but sentence.
	Sentence; [therefore,] sentence.
COLONS	Sentence/General: specifics/list of details.
COMMAS	Sentence, and sentence.
	Introductory phrase containing a verb or more than five words, sentence.
	Transition, sentence.
	Sentence, shifting modifier.
	adjective, adjective noun
	item, item[,] and item
	Sen-, interrupter, -tence.
	noun, describing clause,
	noun specifying clause
	month day, year,
	month year
APOSTROPHES	singular noun's apostrophe
	plural nouns' apostrophe
	It's a contraction.
HYPHENS	adjective-grouping modifier
NUMBERS	one . . . ten, 11 . . .
	1 percent
	$5 million
	on June 1
CAPITALS	Proper Name
	common name

Figure 6-1. Quick tips on punctuation

PUNCTUATION

Period [.]

1. Marks the end of a complete sentence other than a question or exclamation.

2. Is not used for initials of an organization (*USAF*, *IBM*).

3. Is used with abbreviations of words or titles (*a.m.*, *p.m.*, *Dr.*, *Mrs.*).

4. Goes inside quotation marks.

Question Mark [?]

1. Marks the end of a question.

   When do you want to go?

2. Does not mark the end of a rhetorical question that is actually making a request.

   Would you mind completing this form for me.

3. Falls inside or outside quotation marks, depending on the meaning of the sentence.

   She asked, "Do you have time to talk?"

   Is there another chapter besides "Beginnings"?

Exclamation Point [!]

1. Marks the end of a statement of surprise or excitement.

   Wow! We had a great quarter.

2. Should be used sparingly. They can be annoying and lose their impact if overused.

3. Falls inside or outside quotation marks, depending on the meaning of the sentence.

   The sales reps shouted "Yes!"

   Despite all our efforts, we were labeled "losers"!

Colon [:]

1. May introduce a list or series unless "such as," "for example," or some other transitional phrase is used. The colon is usually preceded by a complete sentence.

   We expect these results from the strategy: increased customer base, wider market area, and higher profits.

2. Before an open list (using bullets or numbers), it is no longer necessary to complete the sentence, as long as it flows grammatically into the listed items. Punctuate the list based on its complexity: no marks after single words, commas after short phrases, semicolons after more complex phrases, or periods after full sentences.

   From the strategy, we expected to achieve:
   - *Increased customer base,*
   - *Wider market area,*
   - *Higher profits.*

3. Introduces an explanation, almost the equivalent of "namely," "that is." What is on one side of the colon explains or balances what is on the other side.

   You were right: She is an excellent writer.

4. Introduces a quotation in a more formal way than a comma.

   Code 25, Section 4 states: "The defendant . . ."

5. Do ***not*** insert a colon between parts of the sentence that belong together (subject and verb, verb and complement).

   Incorrect: *Attendees included: Julius, Samuel, and Theresa.*

6. Follows the salutation in a formal letter. In an informal letter, you may use a comma.

   Dear President Simpson:
   Dear Joe,

Semicolon [;]

1. Separates complete sentences when the meaning is closely related. It functions almost as half a comma and half a period.

   If nominated, I will not run; if elected, I will not serve.

2. Precedes a conjunctive adverb (a transitional word such as *also, however, consequently, therefore*) when connecting complete sentences.

Our profits are up; therefore, we are reinstating travel allowances.

3. Functions as a strong comma to separate a series of phrases that have internal commas.

The meeting agenda included reports from Susan Johnson, vice president; Travis Jones, director of marketing; and Cynthia Reynolds, plant superintendent.

Comma [,]

1. Precedes a coordinating conjunction (*and, or, but, so, yet, for*) joining complete sentences.

The traffic light malfunctioned, and the intersection was a free-for-all.

Do not use a comma before *and* unless it separates complete sentences. For strong contrast, you may use a comma before an *or* or *but* that does not separate complete sentences.

We expect to receive your application and a letter of recommendation.

We expected to receive your application, but did not.

2. Separates an introductory clause or phrase with a verb in it from the main sentence.

To explain her plan, Marilyn used charts and graphs.

Because the information was complex, Marilyn used charts and graphs in her presentation.

3. Sets off any introductory phrase of five or more words. With fewer than five words, the comma is optional.

At the end of the very long meeting, we made some quick decisions.

4. Usually follows transitional words or phrases at the beginning of a sentence or surrounds transitions (*In that case, Therefore, i.e.,*) unless they are very short (*Also* or *Then*).

> Commas are "break marks," not "breath marks." Do not insert a comma every time you pause.

Refining

Nevertheless, the cost spiral continues.

Then hit "Enter."

The invoice arrived late, i.e., on the 30th of the month.

5. May separate a dependent clause or modifying phrase at the end of a sentence if there is a noticeable shift in emphasis.

   I have decided to go ahead with the plan, despite my misgivings.

6. Sets off interrupting expressions or explanations.

   Doctors, I think, have insufficient knowledge of acupuncture.

   Mr. Ball, the president for 25 years, was greatly respected.

   We expect, however, to improve our performance.

7. Indicates describing clauses. Describing clauses give more information about the noun, but can be omitted without changing the meaning of the sentence.

   The desk, which is available at several stores, will improve the office appearance. [*Only one desk is being discussed.*]

   Specifying, or essential, clauses are not set off with commas.

   The desk which needs to be moved is in the corner.
   [*There are at least two desks, but only the one in the corner needs to be moved.*]

   Traditional grammar made a distinction between *which* to introduce describing adjective clauses and *that* to introduce specifying adjective clauses. However, current practice no longer makes that distinction. You must look to the meaning to determine whether a modifier describes or specifies.

8. Sets off direct quotations.

   She said, "Please send me a memo."

   Do not use a comma to set off an indirect quotation.

   She said that I should send her a memo.

9. Separates each item in a series. The comma before the *and* at the end of a series may be omitted if the meaning is clear (journalists' style). [*See semicolon for complex series punctuation.*]

   She bought a dress, a pair of sandals, and a purse to match.

10. Separates simple adjectives describing the same noun.

    She wrote a pretty, good report. [*It was pretty and good.*]

    Not: She wrote a pretty good report. [*Neither pretty nor good*]

11. Sets off *yes*, *no*, and *etc.*

    No, I will not agree to meet, talk, etc., until next week.

12. Sets off words of direct address.

    Joe, meet me at the corner.

13. Separates two parts of a geographical location and follows names of states or countries.

    She was born in New York, NY, in 1986.

14. Sets off the year from the month and day. Do not use between month and year only.

    Tuesday, June 10, 2003,   but   *June 2003*

15. No longer follows a year unless the month and day are also stated.

    In 2003 you wrote that . . . but *On July 20, 2003, you wrote . . .*

16. Follows the salutation and complimentary close.

17. Goes inside closing quotation marks.

Dash [—]

 1. In typed text, a dash is two hyphens: --

 2. Indicates an abrupt break. Use it sparingly. The material within dashes is very emphatic.

    The courtroom—that hallowed hall of justice—is too often backlogged.

 3. Can serve like a colon, as a pause before a series. This use is appropriate only in informal or very expressive writing.

    Children can make mischief in any place—on the yard, at school, in church.

Parentheses [( )]

1. Deemphasize material. Information in parentheses is less essential than if set off by commas.

   The minimum fabric overlap requirement of 2 longitudinal wire spaces = 2" (i.e., 1"–2") will not be met.

2. If the parenthetical information is a full sentence and stands alone, the end punctuation is inside the parentheses. However, if the parentheses end a sentence and complete it, the period or other end mark is outside the final parenthesis.

   (See Chapter 5 for a full explanation.)

   While in our city (he has since returned to Los Angeles), the film director shot several commercials about our local attractions.

3. Do not use to explain pronouns.

   Wrong: *He (Jones) was young.*
   Write instead: *Jones was young.*

4. Do not break up a sentence with a long parenthesis because the reader will lose track of the main idea.

Apostrophe [']

1. Indicates noun possession. For a singular noun, add *'s*.

   A week's work, an employee's office, IBM's strategy

2. To form the possessive of plural nouns:

   If the word ends in *-s*, add only an apostrophe:
   the Smiths' house [*not The Smith's*], *the assistants' desks*

   If the plural does not end in *-s*, add an apostrophe and an *-s*:
   women's shoes

3. For nouns ending in *-s*, *-cks*, *-x*, or *-z*, say the word outloud and notice if you are adding an *-s*. If you add *-s* when you say it, add an apostrophe and *-s* when you write it:

   Jesus' parables, the boss's office

4. Do **not** add an apostrophe to personal pronouns.

   his book, its alternative

5. Do use the apostrophe to show indefinite pronouns' possession.

one's hopes, others' opinions

6. Indicates the letters or numbers left out of a contraction.

He didn't do it. The class of '90. It's your move.

7. Do not add an apostrophe for a plural acronym.

We issued three RFPs.

Hyphen [-]

1. Connects adjectives functioning as one-word descriptions and preceding the noun:

out-of-date report, short-term profit, company-owned plane

If the last word is a verb form, the phrase will be hyphenated no matter where it is in the sentence:

The new plane is company-owned.

Exception—If the first word ends in *-ly*, do not use a hyphen: *It was a widely accepted theory.*

2. In a series of phrases sharing a common word, suspend the hyphen on the first and then complete the second hyphenated phrase: *short- and long-term plans*.

3. No longer attaches most prefixes or suffixes: *cooperate, preretirement, coworker, companywide*.

Attaches prefixes or suffixes in a few instances: *all-knowing, pro-ERA, self-made*. Check your dictionary, *The Gregg Reference Manual*, or another standard office reference.

4. Is always used after prefixes before a proper name: *anti-American*.

5. Because of computers' word-wrap function, we rarely divide words at the end of a line. However, if you must, remember these guidelines for word division:

   ■ Divide between syllables.

   ■ Do not divide a one-syllable word or separate a single letter.

Refining

Ellipses [...]

1. Indicate words omitted from quoted text.

2. Do not use, even in casual e-mails, to indicate a pause.

MECHANICS

Numbers [#]

1. Spell out numbers from *one* to *ten*, and use numerals above *ten*: **one . . . ten, 11 . . . .** If numbers above and below *ten* occur in the same sentence, be consistent.

   We ordered copies of the 15 notebooks.

   We ordered 6 copies each of the 15 notebooks.

2. Never start a sentence with a numeral. Spell out the number or rearrange the sentence.

3. Percents always use numerals followed by *percent*, unless in a technical calculation where the % symbol is appropriate.

4. Use numerals in writing about money, measurement, dates, fractions, or other technical data.

5. There is no need to repeat numbers in parentheses [e.g., *ten (10)*] unless the document is a contract or specifications.

Dates

1. Use only numerals for the day, without *st, nd, th*, etc., in normal month, day, year order: *September 1, 200_*

2. Use the *st, nd, th*, etc., if the day precedes the month:

   the 1st of September

Abbreviations [abbr.]

1. Use abbreviations sparingly, especially with words that are normally spelled out:

   December, **not Dec.;** *government,* **not govt.**

2. Most acronyms (letters replacing names) do not use periods:

   IBM, RFP, PC

3. Use periods after the letters in lower case abbreviations:

   a.m., p.m., etc., e.g., i.e.

4. If an abbreviation occurs at the end of the sentence, only one period is needed.

Capitalization [cap]

1. Capitalize proper names, i.e., the unique name of a person or entity:

   Bessie Thompson, the Marketing Department, July, Widget Manufacturing

2. Do not capitalize common nouns, i.e., a generic name:

   my mother, our department, this month, our company

3. Job titles are not capitalized, except in formal documents such as minutes of meetings:

   The manager of the Accounting Department called a meeting for 2:00 p.m.

4. Capitalize the form words but not the structure words in titles and subject lines:

   Subject: Budget Report Due in Two Weeks

5. Capitalize the first word of a sentence. Do not capitalize the first word following a colon unless it begins a full sentence.

6. Capitalize the first word in each item in a list, even if it is a single word.

7. Capitalize only the first word of a complimentary closing:

   Thank you, Very truly yours,

8. For state names in addresses, use the U.S. Postal Service abbreviations with two capitals and no periods: *FL, NY, OK, TX*, and so on.

Practice: Punctuation and Mechanics

Correct all punctuation and mechanics errors in the following sentences. The symbols indicate the primary problem with the sentences.

[,]

1. We plan to use two people entering the same information on a diskette, then a software program will match the entries and produce a list of the ones that don't match.

2. If there is any way I can help please let me know.

3. Although, not much I trust it will help out.

4. Mary Jane in our International Department, has informed us that the Letter of Credit numbers are pre-issued.

5. Keys can be created in the user's own file allowing more efficient data processing.

6. Mr. Brown believes the return was filed in a timely manner, however, the taxpayer has no proof of this.

7. We would like your response to the 6 findings and recommendations noted in our report, and in particular, to the items listed below.

8. Their tanks are on control now and when the tank reaches a certain level a valve opens allowing fuel to flow to the tank.

9. In closing the Architect, Mr. Smith asked that in lieu of an immediate decision or directive as we had originally intended, that some additional time be given for cost analysis and consideration.

[:]

10. This column will cover the three essential elements of unseating an industry leader, spot the opportunity, attack, and cover your backside.

11. They are listed below in order of the farthest East down to the road;

12. These include: air quality, wildlife, land preservation and hazardous waste and many more factors affecting our ecological systems.

[;]

13. The job posting program in itself will entail producing and storing many items on a P.C.; including: the job posting form, log of applicants - placements and results, letters to candidates, and daily updates of statistics.

14. Submit a section showing the design through the building; including connection to the existing building.

[']

15. This amount was to cover taxpayers estimate of any additional tax still owed. At some point between April 1, 200_ and August 10, 200_, taxpayer's believe their return was filed.

16. The assessors' office uses the addition and deletions sheet to reclassify property.

17. Jones who has seven years experience in the small retail business expects the rental trend to dramatically shift to video games.

18. An account executive for Famous Jewelry made a point to memorize his customer's wives' names and special events in their lives such as birthdays and anniversaries.

19. Please, look at this wording and let me know if its ok.

20. ACME assures you of its' utmost commitment to provide you with quality and responsiveness in the products we deliver.

[-]

21. The company has gone to great pains to minimize marketing related expenses and to shift the burden of producing marketing materials to our affiliates.

22. You make several broad based, wide ranging, all encompassing statements without providing details for rational conclusions.

23. I will contact you to set a follow up meeting.

24. The short and long term cost is significant.

25. We would run our pre-approved radio ads "Boxing" and "Travel" using the 40 second version with a 20 second custom tag during the campaign.

[abbr.]

26. The seminar will begin at 8:00 am, and end at 4:00 pm.

27. We would like to meet monthly; eg. the first Tuesday.

[#/date]

28. The project took a total of 5 hours utilizing 10 CSR's at 30 minutes each.

29. There is a three (3) inch open ended pipe in place used to drain the levee.

30. The date of February 21st has been confirmed for the off-site Senior Management meeting from 8:00 am to 12:00 noon.

31. The 5 PC's that were separated from the main ring are running three different operating systems.

32. We plan to extend the lease for a term of Ten (10) years at $20.00 per month on May 21st, 200_.

[cap]

33. periodic check of hard copies will be made to verify inspections. (30 day max.)

34. I plan to follow up on this Firm particularly in regard to ASRP.

35. John will be reviewing our proposal with the President of his company during the first week of March, 200_.

36. We intend to determine the effect of the marketing effort on:

    + telephone responses

    + sales increase

    + short term profit

37. She is currently being trained on Tort Claims, Garnishments, Checking out Documents, Retrieving items from the vault and scanning documents.

38. You spoke with our Fraud Investigator Craig & Craig indicated to me that you thought that you had already paid for these charges.

39. if you could check this for me i would appreciate it.
                              thanks

40. We know you will enjoy seeing our lovely City.

Practice: Punctuation

Insert the correct punctuation and mechanics in the memo in Figure 6-2.

to: all employees

from: lee winn

subject: corporate policy

date: july 6th 200_

it is official company policy that each branch must complete proper reports this policy is further outlined in company procedure 2250 in addition ms jones our president said in her memo of may 10 2003 branch reports are the most important indicator of our companys success according to our records you have not forwarded reports on time have filled out reports incorrectly and have ignored our previous requests for prompt reports to insure that your july report is in my office by the august 10 deadline mark your calendar today the jones company needs your cooperation in sending prompt correct monthly reports may we count on your cooperation

thanks

lee

Figure 6-2. Punctuation practice

Practice: Proofreading

Correct all errors in the letter in Figure 6-3.

MAJOR MANUFACTURING, INC.

P.O. Box 231
Capital City, California 93452
832.555.9756

August 18 200_

Samantha Johnson
The Leading Company
P.O Box 3456
Central City, Ark. 55512

Dear Ms Johnson;

In regards to the recent Request for Verification of Employment that you completed on Tim Swanson. We are in need of additional information. It is required that we have box 11 (Probability of Continued Employment) filed in.

If you desire you can use something like we can not comment or we are an at will company. You should fill in the form we sent, otherwise we can not process your request.

Thank you for your prompt response to this. If you have farther questions please don't hesitate to call.

Thank You,

Amy Sanders
Loan processor

Figure 6-3. Proofreading practice

WORKSPACE

Practice: Major Refining

Correct all the problems in the letter in Figure 6-4. You may make any revisions or formatting changes you wish to improve its readability.

ALL AMERICAN TELEPHONE COMPANY
SunCity, Florida

Mr. A. B. Reader
1104 Apple Avenue
Quality City, Florida 11111-2222

Dear Mr. Reader:

As per our conversation of Dec. 13th, I am sending you a copy of my recommended changes for your long distance communication needs. The services you are currently using from AATC is antiquated, in regards to your changing calling paterns, it is not as flexable as the way you call. Therefore AATC has committed to its customers to keep them in the forefront of ever changing technology. It is this committment that has made AATC reevaluate all of its services, and make necessary enhancements to them. In order to keep your company using the most economical services that AATC has to offer.

By taking Advantage of these new enhancements your company will benefit in five (5) different discount areas,
1) NPA = highest calling AreaCode = 10% discount to the highest called areacode each month.
2) FNO = highest called Country = 10% discount to the highest called country each month.
3) Intra Company = all calls made between company locations, or all calling card cals back to main company location = 20% discount on all of these calls.
4) Volume Discounts = Tapered between 5% and 15% = depending upon total volume used each month.
5) Flex Option Discount = an extra discount based on time and monthly committments to AATC tapered between an extra 3% and 8.5%. Also the convenience on only having to pay one bill, because this service allows your company to tie together all of its location into one monthly bill. Thereby allowing you to take advantage of something that previously only very large companies sush as "Sears" or "Avis" could take advantage of.

I have enclosed a short comparison of how you company is being billed now and what it is costing, as compared to the new service billing enhancements. To have the New Enhancements implemented please contact me at 1 800-906-1111 ext. 7654 or 504 323-0000.

Sincerely

James Jones

Figure 6-4. Major refining practice

WORKSPACE

Corrected Self-Assessment (p. 154)

Judy Smith and **I** [*pronoun form*] **were** [*subject-verb agreement*] discussing the suspension of employees when they take an in-service [*hyphen*] withdrawal of the Investment Plus or Thrift Plan. Judy would like to know what procedures for the group **are** [*subject-verb agreement*] in place for Tom Johnson or [*unnecessary contrast*] the **P**ayroll **D**epartment [*proper name*], etc., [*comma after etc.*] to start and stop a suspension.

I recently sent a memo to Susan Thompson regarding an [*an before vowel sound*] employee currently suspended in the Thrift Plan [*proper name*] so that **his** [*noun-pronoun agreement*] suspension would not be interrupt**ed** [*verb form*] **due** [*spelling*] to the changes in the **p**lan [common noun]**.** [*comma splice*] I've attached a copy of the memo sent to Susan for your [*possessive pronoun*] information.

Also, [*comma after transition*] do we continue to **input** [*spelling*] the "Thrift Plan Date" on **the** [*omitted word*] **Benefits Screen 3** [*screen name; not possessive*] when the [*omitted word*] employee initially joins the plan**?** [*question*] If we are to continue**,** [*fragment*] how do we know when an employee joins the plan [*common noun*] so we can input this date **into** [*spelling*] the program?

Thanks for your help in **these** [*agreement*] matters.

The original had 25 errors. How did you do?

Missed 0 to 2—Great job, grammar guru.
Missed 3 to 5—Pretty sharp eye, but you need to concentrate.
Missed 6 to 8—You're okay but a little rusty. This chapter will help.
Missed 9 or more—Now is your chance to improve those proofreading skills.

Practice

Tiger Woods hits the driving range or putting green until dark *after* ending most tournament rounds. Even if he leads the tournament, he is constantly reinforcing his skills. That may be why he's the best. Greatness comes with practice.

This section presents these opportunities to help you hone your writing skills to reach greatness:

- A checklist to use in guiding and reviewing your writing process.

- Real workplace scenarios that require you to apply the strategies presented in the book. Your instructor may assign some of these, or you may want to do them for extra skill-building. You may be working on several assignments at the same time, just as you might be in different stages of the writing process while writing several documents simultaneously at work.

- More editing and proofreading exercises on real workplace documents. The proofreading examples have been doctored; no one would make all those errors!

- Possible revisions for the practice exercises from the Editing and Refining chapters. Compare your answers with these revisions; yours may be better.

Good writers are not necessarily born with talent. They work at it. So, when you practice the strategies of effective writing, have fun, work hard, keep practicing, and continue to improve. It's a rewarding game.

CHAPTER 7—PRACTICE

Practice

READER-FRIENDLY WRITING CHECKLIST

In **Planning** and **Organizing**, have you:

■ Thought about your readers and purpose?

■ Stated your main idea in the first paragraph?

■ Arranged your key points logically?

■ Mentioned the specific action you want?

Have you **Written** paragraphs that:

■ Begin with strong topic sentences?

■ Present specific details to explain your key points?

■ Stick to one topic?

■ Use clear transitions and logical order?

■ Employ white space and other design features to emphasize points?

In **Editing**, have you:

■ Checked for spelling and precise word choice?

■ Watched your jargon and chosen a direct, personal voice?

■ Edited for conciseness by choosing strong, action verbs and pruning extra words?

In **Refining**, have you:

■ Checked grammatical correctness (fragments, comma splices, subject-verb agreement, pronoun reference)?

■ Reviewed spelling, punctuation, and mechanics?

■ Set up a format for the final document that will make the reader's job easy?

PRACTICE SCENARIOS

The best way to gain proficiency is to practice your writing skills as if you're in a real situation. The following scenarios are typical of the writing many people do at work. Choose one or more to work on.

You may want to hold your developing document(s) in a folder, applying the principles as you complete each chapter. Just as in an office, you may be working on several documents at the same time. Remember to follow these steps as you practice reader-friendly writing.

Based on your workplace experience, create details for each scenario.

Planning

- Analyze the audiences, their informational needs, their levels of expertise, and their potential uses of the document.

- Define the purpose of your document. What do you want to achieve?

- Brainstorm possible content. What information might you want to include?

Organizing

- Using your brainstormed list of possible content, decide what information to include and what to leave out based on your audience(s) and purpose.

- Develop a blueprint by grouping related details and identifying the key points you want to make.

- Arrange the paragraph topics in a logical order.

- Draft a main idea.

- Outline an introduction and conclusion.

Writing

- Working from your blueprint, write a draft document.

- Put your key points at the beginning of each paragraph.

■ Focus paragraphs on one point per paragraph.

■ Arrange details in logical order within paragraphs.

■ Add transitions when needed.

■ Decide if you need any open lists, section headings, or captioned figures.

■ Create a clear subject line.

Editing

Revise your draft document for:

■ Precise word choice and spelling,

■ No formal, complex vocabulary,

■ Jargon only when appropriate and defined, if necessary,

■ Concrete and specific, rather than abstract, words,

■ Wordy phrases pruned out,

■ Strong action verbs.

Refining

Proofread your draft for:

■ Complete sentences,

■ Correct sentence punctuation,

■ No long, rambling sentences,

■ Interesting sentence variety,

■ No problems with verb forms, subject-verb agreement, or pronoun usage,

■ Correct punctuation,

■ Correct mechanics,

■ Proper document format.

Scenario One—Solving a Problem

You and your boss have been discussing a problem in your department for quite a while. Together, you have considered several options for solving the problem, one of which is very obvious, the first thing everyone thinks of as a solution. But you have decided to try a less obvious solution that will cost a sizable amount to implement. You and your boss agree it offers a permanent solution and thus is worth the cost.

Now that you have agreed on the solution, your boss says, "Send me an e-mail about that."

Your Task—Create an e-mail that will meet your boss's needs. Using your own workplace experiences, invent the details: What's the problem? What are the optional solutions? What solution did you choose? What is the cost? Then decide what information your boss wants and what she will do with it, write and edit the e-mail.

Scenario Two—Announcing Training

Your team has asked for training in effective presentation skills. Everyone has mixed feelings: a strong desire to improve this critical skill, but also some butterflies about being videotaped. You have found an excellent instructor and made all the arrangements for the two-day training session. Now you need to inform your team about the details and reduce their nervousness so that everyone will attend.

Your Task—Based on your workplace experience, write an e-mail announcing the training. What details do your team members need about the session itself? What does the class cover? Who is the instructor and what are his qualifications? What benefits can your team members expect to gain?

Scenario Three—Answering a Complaint

You have received a complaint from a very polite but irritated customer. After buying your product or service for more than 20 years, she has had three bad experiences in a row. All were different problems, so you cannot identify a single quality issue to address. Your check with the appropriate departments gives you little help. Everyone you talked to was too busy to give you an adequate explanation about why such problems could have happened or how they might be solved. Without much information, you still need to answer your faithful customer, who may be ready to buy from your competitor.

Your Task—Using details from your own experience, write a letter that will retain your customer and her loyalty to your company. Invent details about the service or product, the problems she encountered, possible causes, and possible ways to respond to her. How might you respond? What should you not do or say?

Scenario Four—Creating a Desk Procedure

You are going on vacation for two weeks—a Caribbean cruise that you have planned for a year, followed by several days in sunny Florida. You are really excited, except you dread returning to a pile of work. A relatively new employee is willing to handle your routine tasks while you're gone if you prepare clear instructions for him to follow. You do not have written desk procedures now, but decide this is a good reason to develop some.

Your Task—Create a procedure for one important task from your current or a previous job that must be completed daily or weekly. Include any details that someone unfamiliar with the task would need to know. Be careful about using jargon.

Scenario Five—Investigating Bad Financial Data

Your group has been receiving conflicting financial data on your primary product or service. Some mid-month computer runs project results that are close to your sales forecasts for the month. But the month-end reports show that your group fell significantly short of projections. After several months of this situation, you and two coworkers are certain there must be a problem with one report or the other. Your manager has asked you to research the problem and prepare a report. Assume that you and your coworkers have completed your analysis of the problem, have identified the problem, and are ready to recommend a solution.

Your Task—Based on your work experience, develop details for the scenario: your product or service, the financial details (costs, number of sales, revenues, etc.), a potential problem that could cause reporting errors, possible causes, and any possible solutions.

■ Create a blueprint for a three-page report, plus appendices.

■ Write and edit the Overview section for the report.

■ If you wish, write and edit the entire report.

Practice: Selling Your Services

The president of a national association received the letter in Figure 7-1 from someone offering his services to handle mass mailings—not a bad idea. However, the letter was so unfocused and littered with errors, it did not merit an answer. Reorganize the ideas, write a draft, and revise to create a clear, correct final draft. Remember to focus your sales letter on WIIFM—What's In It For Me, the reader.

Association of Professional Consultants
Attention: Mary Norton
4376 S. Trenton
Central City, ST 56873
(310) 555-3245

Dear Mary,

First I would like to start off with simply I can do your form letters with the mailing labels. I can furnish the envelopes and the mailing labels and the paper for the letters. I would like the letters to basically have the same body of the letter (and if you need some extra notation to a particular person to have it written in red or under-lined in red. Or if it's a certain group that's suppose to have a certain type of letter to let me know. Basically all it is is instructions!).

I can also type any certain type of forms you need so all you have to do is fill them in for the office. Anything from the basics to whatever you need to make you save time.

If you have people in my area that are willing to mail their manuscript to me; I can type their work for them on perforated computer paper. Plus I would need their number in case I don't understand their writing.

Fees are based in the time of the job. A full week not including postage can cost two hundred and forty dollars and of course you don't have to worry about deductions because I am a business owner but because of the state I'll have to charge you tax! If I finish a job before the week is up I will call and let you know that the price is lowered. Also I would like half of the fee before starting the job and the rest after the job is over. A problem for small business owners! +

I would like to have a two week notice; but that can be flexible! If you have any other questions please feel free to call! I'll enclose some different types of letter heads that you can choose from or if you have some ideas of your own that works best for your office let me know!

Yours truly,

Joseph A. Samson

P.S. + The tax rate for type of services is 7 ¾!
Enclosure: Types of letterhead

Figure 7-1. Unsuccessful sales letter

<u>WORKSPACE</u>

Practice: Formatting for Readability

Some people claim that legal documents, to be consistent with professional norms, cannot change. Long sentences, complex verbiage, and packed paragraphs are required. This is not true. Try rewriting the reader-unfriendly Notice of Hearing in Figure 7-2. Use plain English and an open format to clarify what accounting rule changes will be considered at the hearing.

NOTICE OF HEARING

Notice is hearby given that pursuant to sections 15.08(5) and 442.01(2), State Stats., the Accounting Examining Board, Department of Regulation and Licensing, will hold a public hearing on Conference Room 1750 A of the Washington Square Building, 8723 East Lincoln Street, in the city of Centreville, State, on the 13th day of May 13, 200_, at 10:00 a.m. to consider the repeal and recreation of Accy 1.101(1), 1.201(1), 1.202(1) and 1.204(1) to modify editorially the rules on independence, general standards, auditing standards and technical standards, respectively; the amendment of Accy. 1.201(2), 1.501(2)(b), and 6.03(1) (intro) to reflect statutory provision that conviction for a crime must be substantially related to the practice of accounting to be relevant; the adoption of Accy.1.101(2)(f) and 1.504(2) to interpret the effect of actual or threatened litigation on independence and the application of the rule on incompatible occupations, respectively; the repeal of Chapter Accy.2, Conduct of Hearings, Pleadings and Procedure, since these provisions are now defined in the statutes; the repeal of Accy. 7.02 through 7.06, recreation of Accy.7.02 and 7.03 and renumbering Accy.7.07, 7.08 and 7.09 to explain the education requirement for certified public accountants and define an accounting major where not completed as part of a Bachelor's or higher degree; the renumbering of Accy. Chapter 8, Public Access to Records, 8.01, 8.02, 8.03, 8.04 and 8.05 to Chapter Accy.2, Public Access to Records, 2.01, 2.02, 2.03, 2.04 and 2.05, respectively; and the adoption of Accy. 6.03(1)(d) and (e) to include substantial relationship to the practice of accounting and bondability as items to be considered in determining if an individual lacks good moral character.

A copy of the proposed rules to be considered may be obtained from the Accounting Examining Board, Department of Regulation and Licensing, 8723 East Lincoln Street, Centreville, State 76458 (Telephone 877-324-3020), upon request.

Figure 7-2. Reader-unfriendly Notice of Hearing

<u>**WORKSPACE**</u>

Practice: Editing for Clarity and Conciseness

The letter from a business owner to a banker in Figure 7-3 shows the excessive formality that some writers believe they need to use in business correspondence. Can you translate what the writer was trying to say?

May 31, 200_

Felicia Perez
Credit Department
Hometown Bank, NA
Hometown, UT 65940

Dear Ms. Perez:

You will please find attached those financial reports from the Super Company that you had recently requested of our controller, Sarah O'Hare. Please accept my apologies for the delay that has occurred in their being forwarded to you. I assure you that we will be more punctual on future occasions.

As I have not yet had the pleasure of making your personal acquaintance, I shall advantage this opportunity to share with you that I would welcome the occasion to address any questions that you might have in regard to the operation of Super Company. Further to that, I very much want that you should have as thorough an understanding of our situation as it is your desire to maintain, and hope that as it may be convenient for you to do so that we might speak briefly in order to determine the process by which to best facilitate such on a going forward basis.

Thank you for your interest and support of the Super Company. I shall look forward to the opportunity to speak with you.

Respectfully,

Jared Thompson
Shop Manager

Figure 7-3. Old-fashioned, formal style

WORKSPACE

Practice: Editing for a "You" Attitude

The solicitation letter in Figure 7-4 was sent with the best intent—to line up prizes for the company holiday party. Donors would receive some benefits in advertising and traffic at their restaurants. Unfortunately, the letter's strong focus on "I" makes the letter sound self-serving. It also is wordy. Rewrite it to focus on "you" and the benefits your restaurant would receive by donating gift certificates.

Dear Manager/Owner:

Hi, my name is Audry Alessa and I am an Accountant at Apex Company in Central City. We are approaching our annual Holiday Party for our accounting staff here at the Business Center and in order to make the party a successful one, we are soliciting for prizes to give away to our accountants who attend the Holiday Celebration.

I am sending this letter to what we consider the best restaurants in the Central City area – those that have the best food, service, atmosphere, and that best represent Central City.

We have concluded that gift certificates from restaurants such as yours would be the best type of prizes for our Holiday celebration, not only for the attendees, but for the restaurants as well. Everyone enjoys a good meal, and the donation of certificates would provide relatively cheap advertisement for your restaurant that would reach our Accountants here in Central City. (We have approximately 1000 people employed here in Central City.)

I appreciate your time and consideration, and hope that you can help make our Holiday celebration a great one with donations of a gift certificate.

A stamped and addressed envelope has been included for any responses/replies that you may have.

Thanks,

Audry Alessa
Staff Accountant
Holiday Celebration Committee

Figure 7-4. "I" versus "You" focus

<u>WORKSPACE</u>

Practice: Having Fun with Editing

Even the pros need editing. Identify the problem with each of the
following real goofs from newspapers. Then rewrite the sentences
so that they make sense.

1. "Coach Mike Krzyzewski asked some of his players over to the house for dinner one day last spring, then barbecued himself."

2. "This is the third marriage of the groom. He has also been through World War II."

3. "Why would a young mother wait nine hours in line to get front row tickets to a show? The Mighty Morphine Power Rangers, friends."

4. "The dead man was described as white, aged between 30 and 40, with an Irish accent."

5. "From now on, police will pick up road-killed animals, not Public Works employees."

6. "Spike Lee says his new movie 'Malcolm X' ends in the townships of South Africa, not the Harlem ballroom where the black nationalist leader was assassinated for artistic reasons."

7. "Garden club members heard a talk on bugs and roaches. A large number were present."

8. "Seven pages of the biography are devoted to revelations about Coco Chanel's habit of cooling champagne by pouring it over a block of ice, her rock crystal collection, her brown pillows and her paneled closets."

9. "Japanese tabloids are all atwitter that the wife of Crown Prince Naruhito, whose years-long search for a bride was exhaustively chronicled, might soon be a father."

10. "NOTICE: I wish to thank anyone who so kindly assisted in my husband's death."

Practice: Proofreading

Using standard proofreading marks, correct all the errors in
punctuation, spelling, and mechanics in the letter in Figure 7-5.

3 January 200_

Mr. John Smith, president
Smith Engineering Inc.
P.o. Box 1111
Our Town, Texas 56734

    Re: Your account No. 23546; Creek Flood

Dear Smith;

    Enclosed herewith please find our check for $412.38. Which is payment in full for for
your services in the above stated matter. WE appreciate you excellent counsel and advise
during the investigation and subsequent trail in Center City, and look forward to working
with you again.

Should you have any questions or comments please don't hesitate to give us a call, my
number is (345) 555-7645.

                  Sincerely,

                  Amanda H Lee
                  Secreatry to Sam Jones

Figure 7-5. Practice proofreading

<u>WORKSPACE</u>

Practice: Revising for Clarity and Correctness

Using standard proofreading marks, revise the letter in Figure 7-6
to improve word choice and to correct all errors.

Manager of Sales
The Hospitality Inn
6754 west Highway
Main Draw, ST 96784

Dear Manger,

I want to clarify a few items that did not met with out satisfaction during the Seminar we
held at the Hospitality hotel on July 4th. To alleviate any future problems some explanation
is due.

1. Several items such as the flipcharts, markers, microphones etc., which were to be set
    up no later than 7:30 AM were not ready. Four to five trips were made to the front desk
    before we finally got service. Our meeting was delayed passed 8:30 AM..
2. We were no informed of the additional meeting room until mid morning. This caused
    confusion. The arrangments were very disorganized.

3. We were not informed the luncheon would be waiter served meal. The arrival of the
    meal was over thirty minutes late.

4. I recieved complaints from the entire group including upper management who were
    very disappointed over the meal.

Should we ever decide to do business with The Hospitality again I do hope these problem
wont be repeated.

Thank You for Your Attention,

Robert Clark
Training Manager

Figure 7-6. Practice in revision

WORKSPACE

Practice: Revising to Clarify Purpose

Here is how the original author revised her unclear Second
Request memo.

Original

Interoffice Correspondence

Date: November 27, 200_

To: John Legal

From: Alice Accounting

Subject: APEX LABORATORIES (Second Request)

The work performed on the above contract was started before the contract was executed;
thus it is required that the authority to do this be appropriately documented. Please send
this to my attention so that I can attach it to the contract.

This contract is over $50,000, and because of the changes made on this standard form, a
preexecution review by the Legal Department should have been completed and documented on or with the contract. Because this contract is for $100,000, insurance verifica-
tion is required.

If you have any questions, my extension is 5436.

cc: Contract File

Revised

Interoffice Correspondence

Date: November 27, 200_

To: John Legal

From: Alice Accounting

Subject: APEX LABORATORIES (Second Request)

Please send the following items to my attention as soon as possible:

1.   Authorization to start the project before the contract was executed.

2.   A pre-execution review by the Legal Department.

3.   Insurance verification.

If you have any questions, please call me at ext. 5436.

cc: Contract File

ANSWERS TO CHAPTER 5, "EDITING" PRACTICE EXERCISES

Jargon Workplace Application (p. 112)

1. Witnesseth: That parties to these presents, each in consideration of the undertakings, promises and agreements on the part of the other herein contained, have undertaken, promised, and agreed and do hereby undertake, promise and agree, each for itself, its successors and assigns, as follows:

   The parties agree, and commit those who follow to the same agreement.

2. *Ann Landers' column quoted a bulletin sent to parents describing a new Houston education program:*

   "Our school's cross-graded, multi-ethnic, individualized learning program is designed to enhance the concept of an open-ended learning program with emphasis on a continuum of multi-ethnic, academically enriched learning, using the identified intellectually gifted child as the agent or director of his own learning. Major emphasis is on cross-graded, multi-ethnic learning with the main objective being to learn respect for the uniqueness of a person."

   This new program gives bright children from different racial and ethnic backgrounds the opportunity to learn at their own pace, without traditional grade barriers. Major goals are to enhance learning and learn respect for others' unique talents.

3. *From a Forum address on economic and financial management:*

   "A slow-up of the slowdown is not as good as an upturn of the downcurve, but it is better than either a speedup of the slowdown or a deepening of the downcurve—and it suggests the climate is right for an adjustment of the readjustment.

   "Turning to unemployment, we find a definite decrease in the rate of increase—which shows there is a letting up of the letdown. If the slowdown should speed up, the decrease in the rate of increase of unemployment would turn into an increase in the rate of decrease of unemployment.

   "We expect a leveling-off—referred to on Wall Street as bumping along rock bottom—sometime this winter. This will be followed by a gentle pickup, then a faster pickup, a slow-down of the pickup, and finally a leveling off in the spring."

   Economic conditions—including unemployment—are improving slowly. There may be some ups and downs, but the trend is positive.

4. He was proceeding to install pedestrian heads on mast arm poles at the southwest corner.

   He was installing walk/wait signs at the southwest corner.

5. As lit capacity is eliminated from the market and the long-haul carriers bring their guns to bear on the metro marketplace, which will provide on-ramps to their high capacity cores, we predict an uptick in the competitive telecom marketplace will unfold.

   The telecommunications will become more competitive as [not sure what this means!].

Formal Style Practice (p. 116)

1. The troop leader told his men that "the movement to the new station will be implemented by means of wheeled, gas-operated vehicles."

   The troops will move to the new station in trucks.

2. Illumination is required to be extinguished on these premises.

   Turn out the lights.

3. This construction will encourage the use of leg power for vertical pedestrian circulation.

   A staircase in a shopping mall.

4. Packing is always an issue, whether in the air or ground, you must have enough for your expedition to accommodate your necessities.

   Packing is a problem because you need the essentials when you travel.

5. If you should have any questions or comments, please feel free to contact myself at your convenience. Once again thanks for your cooperation and support. It has been a pleasure dealing with your organization and our relationship shall continue to strengthen.

   Please call if you have questions. We appreciate your continued cooperation and look forward to strengthening our relationship.

Editing Practice: Figure 5-4. Inflated Style (p. 119)

Dear David:

Enclosed please find the above referenced written Consent for your execution. It is required that we request your signature, your obtainment of the signature of Patterson O. Smithfield, and the subsequent restoration of the original document to myself. I will then be responsible for the transmission of this Consent to the remainder of the Board of Directors for their respective approbations.

Revised

Dear David:

Please sign the enclosed consent and have Patterson O. Smithfield sign it also. Then return the form to me so I can send the consent to the board of directors for their approval.

"You" Focus Practice: Figure 5-7 (p. 122)

July 30, 200_

Walter Lee
5489 River lane
City, ST 78957

Mr. Lee,

In order to add Jamie to your account I need you both to please sign the enclosed signature card. I need you to sign in three places, once on the front by your name and twice on the back by the highlighted X's. Then I just need Jamie's signature one time on the front of the card by the highlighted X. I have also provided a postage-paid envelope for you to return the signature card at your earliest convenience.

If you have any questions or concerns please feel free to call. I have included my business card with the branch number. Thank you.

Sincerely,

Customer Service Representative

Revised

Dear Mr. Lee,

To add Jamie to your account, please sign the enclosed signature card in three places: once on the front by your name and twice on the back by the highlighted Xs. Jamie should sign one time on the front of the card by the highlighted X. Please return the signed card in the enclosed envelope.

If you have any questions, please call. My branch number is on the enclosed business card. Thank you.

Sincerely,

Customer Service Representative

Clarity Practice (p. 127)

The point is to invent specific details rather than vague, abstract terms.

1. The cost of the equipment is too high.

   The mixer costs $50 more than comparable equipment sold by competitors.

2. The stock market is off.

   The New York Stock Exchange average dropped 200 points today.

3. What he needs is some kind of disciplinary treatment.

   He needs 30 days in the county jail.

4. They had no one good way of doing things and it took a lot of time getting things done.

   Their quality control processes did not exist, so manufacturing wasted 300 work hours a month reworking parts.

Clear Pronoun Reference Practice (p. 127)

First, circle every "this" in the following paragraph and see whether you can tie each one clearly to the noun it refers to. If not, edit the sentence to make the reference clear, either by changing the text or inserting the missing noun after "this."

Implementing vendor specific validations will decrease error/rejection rates, necessitating *fewer* supplements and fewer provisioning/vendor communications. *This validation process* will decrease both order cost and order time. As *this* is an intensive process, requiring thorough requirements analysis for each specific vendor, *this change* will only be implemented for our major trading partners, the eight regional suppliers. *This process* will also allow us greater applicability of our service agreements, as *these* are valid only for clean (error-free) orders.

Editing Practice: Figure 5-12 (p. 133)

THE PURPOSE FOR THIS FORM IS TO ALLOW ACCOUNTING DEPARTMENT PERSONAL TO SUBMIT TO THE EMPLOYEE SURVEY TASK FORCE SOME SUGGESTIONS AND SOLUTIONS TO THE LISTED ATTENDANCE AND MORALE CONCERNS. ALL INPUT RECEIVED BACK WILL BE TAKEN INTO CONSIDERATION WHEN THE FINAL ACTION PLAN IS DRAWN UP AND SUBMITTED TO THE EXECUTIVE COMMITTEE. IN ADDITION TO THIS FORM, THERE WILL BE SEVERAL SMALLER MEETINGS SET UP TO RECEIVE ANY ADDITIONAL INPUT (SEE ATTACHED SCHEDULE OF MEETINGS). THE DEADLINE FOR SUBMITTING INPUT TO THE FINAL ACTION PLAN IS FEBRUARY 16.   [89 words]

Revised

Please use this form to submit your ideas to the Employee Survey Task Force to resolve the Accounting Department's attendance and morale concerns. We will consider all suggestions before submitting the final Action Plan to the Executive Committee. In addition, you may attend a small meeting to share your ideas (see attached schedule). Our deadline for receiving your input is January 16. [59 words]

Passive to Active Practice (p. 135)

Rewrite these passive sentences so they have active verbs:

1. Checks presented for payment must be approved by GNMA.

   GNMA must approve checks for payment. [actor first]

2. A training manual or handout is provided for each participant.

   Each participant receives a training manual or handout. [new verb]

3. The analyst is required to make determinations of the sample volume for initial use.

   The analyst must determine sample volume for initial use. [strong auxiliary, strong verb]

4. It was determined there was a need to educate and inform our employees about industry issues.

   We need to educate our employees about industry issues. [remove empty sentence openings and redundancy]

Editing for Strong Verbs Practice (p. 135)

1. The age range of children admitted to the Shelter is from birth to 17.

   Children in the Shelter range in age from birth to 17.

2. This was an occurrence that was unforeseen by the company and was outside of their control.

   The company could not control this unforeseen occurrence.

3. There are some overall concepts that represent a different approach than the current system.

   Some general concepts differ from the current system.

4. In order to allow for an adequate evaluation, a sufficient amount of time is required.

   An adequate evaluation requires sufficient time.

5. Upon clicking on the icon with your remote, a second page with detailed information is displayed.

   Clicking on the icon with your remote displays a second page with detailed information.

6. It seems we are faced with a serious issue.

   We face a serious issue.

7. Another reason for the improvement in Total Market Share was the increase in the industry attrition.

   Total Market Share also improved because of increased industry attrition.

8. This section should be reviewed prior to the installation of the antenna.

   Review this section before installing the antenna.

9. Before proceeding, it is recommended, the user(s) read and understand each section.

   Before proceeding, the user(s) should read and understand each section.

Editing Practice (p. 136)

1. We are in receipt of a Fifty dollar, $50., money order payable to General Utility Company.

   We received a $50 money order payable to General Utility Company.

2. My situation is that I have a request from Express Service for this service.

   I have a request from Express Service for this service.

3. If there were any way to consolidate these accounts, month-end reconcilement would be greatly simplified.

   Consolidating these accounts would greatly simplify month-end reconcilement.

4. I do feel that we need to continue the verification process that currently exists to ensure we are delivering an accurate instrument back to the field locations.

   We do need to continue the current verification process to ensure we are delivering an accurate instrument to the field.

5. The survey was targeted at people who live in Austin, Texas, and information was gathered about their shopping habits.

    The survey targeting people in Austin, Texas, gathered information about their shopping habits.

6. There are a few customers whom we were unable to locate in our database through a name search.

    We were unable to locate a few customers in our database through a name search.

7. Our company is a leader in the area of market research.

    Our company is a leader in market research.

8. In order to sell effectively, it is important to understand your customers.

    To sell effectively, you must understand your customers.

9. A notice will be distributed to all employees concerning the Summer Program.

    All employees will receive a notice concerning the Summer Program.

Editing Practice (p. 138)

Over the past few months, it has come to our attention that several of the district locations do not currently utilize these statements. Our understanding is that there are alternative sources of the same information (e.g., the Cumulative file) that many locations access through various computer extractions. Apparently, these extractions are providing the various locations with cost information sufficient to meet their needs. Accordingly, for the purpose of determining if issuance of the statements can be discontinued, we are asking that you review the usefulness of our Detail Cost statements to the Production Department. Removal of the requirements for issuance of such statements might possibly result in elimination of what appears to be a duplication of efforts on the part of our Department.   [123 words]

Revised

Recently we realized that several district locations do not use these statements. They can find the same information in other sources (e.g., the Cumulative file) through computer extractions that give enough cost information to meet their needs. Therefore, please review the usefulness of our Detail Cost statements to the Production Department. Not issuing them might eliminate a duplication of effort.   [60 words]

Word Form Practice (p. 147)

1. Part of the chorus went, "How *bizarre*, how *bizarre*."

2. He also informed me that "Roscoe" was *misspelled*.

3. If you have any questions in the *meantime*, please give me a call at 555-4576.

4. The moving of this bed is *scarring* the walls and the wood doors in the station.

5. For the most part, folk culture depicts rural people in extremely *tight-knit families* with strong clan ties.

6. Superintendents gave a brief update regarding the *status* of the condition of current projects.

7. By finding other *economic* means to raise revenue in a more efficient way, the governor could *be in a better position* to push his educational reform package.

8. The court accepted the following allegations as true in *rendering* its decision:

9. DOT-regulated machines and *horsepower* are *affected*.

10. People *sign* up but fail to show up for the class.

11. At the end of the purge cycle, which lasts 3 *minutes*, the light will come on.

12. Remove *un*necessary clothing.

ANSWERS TO CHAPTER 6, "REFINING" PRACTICE EXERCISES

Fragment Practice (p. 156)

1. After she left my office. I found the file she had been looking for.

    After she left my office, I found the file she had been looking for.

2. Per your telephone conversation with Susan Smith about your above mentioned account.

When you discussed your above-mentioned account with Susan Smith, you said that . . .

3. The error having been corrected.

The error has been corrected.

4. Acknowledging receipt of your letter dated May 14, 200_.

We have received your letter dated May 14, 200_.

5. They will listen to a problem and hear you out, before trouble shooting. Great qualities for any team.

They will listen to a problem and hear you out before troubleshooting – great qualities for any team.

Sentence Errors Practice (p. 158)

1. They shipped more than we ordered, I don't know why they would issue a credit.

They shipped more than we ordered. I don't know why they would issue a credit.

2. I hope to receive your answer next week if not I'll call you then we can discuss the project.

I hope to receive your answer next week. If not, I'll call you so we can discuss the project.

3. In addition to a major commitment in terms of personnel, space, telephone lines and equipment; managing an ongoing telemarketing sales effort requires skill and dedication.

In addition to requiring a major commitment in terms of personnel, space, telephone lines and equipment, managing an ongoing telemarketing sales effort requires skill and dedication.

4. I would like two sets of pictures of your establishment. One for my files and one to send in to an architectural magazine.

I would like two sets of pictures of your establishment: one for my files and one to send in to an architectural magazine.

5. The elevator is not running again—it must need a new electrical system.

The elevator is not running again. It must need a new electrical system.

Sentence Focus Practice (p. 160)

1. According to our station attendant on duty at the time of the accident, Mr. Jones saw a girl that he knew and sped away from the pumps in great haste in order to catch up with her and was certainly not paying attention to safe driving when he collided with the very obvious utility pole.

   According to our station attendant on duty at the time of the accident, Mr. Jones saw a girl that he knew and sped away from the pumps in great haste to catch up with her. He was certainly not paying attention to safe driving when he collided with the very obvious utility pole.

2. Our board room has an SL-1 phone and should not be unplugged.

   Our board room has an SL-1 phone, which should not be unplugged.

3. If so, are the calculations the same, and in addition to the reports enclosed, what additional reports are necessary to assist management in controlling inventories?

   If so, are the calculations the same? In addition to the enclosed reports, what additional reports are necessary to assist management in controlling inventories?

4. Go into the control panel and click the "modem Icon" and view which manufacturer of your modem and then return to "Msmail" under the connect menu and select "Communications" and then pick a script that has the name similar to your modem manufacturer and click ok and try again.

   Go into the control panel, click the "modem Icon," and view the manufacturer of your modem. Then return to "Msmail" under the connect menu and select "Communications." Then pick a script that has the name similar to your modem manufacturer, click OK, and try again.

Dangling Modifier Practice (p. 162)

1. Central Technology's Year End is June 30, 200_, ALL CLASSES prior to this date must be turned in before June 29, 200_, to be eligible for assistance.

   Central Technology's Year End is June 30, 200_. To be eligible for assistance, you must turn in all earlier classes before June 29, 200_.

2. Hoping to improve the group's safety record, the training sessions were scheduled for five consecutive weeks.

   Hoping to improve the group's safety record, we scheduled the training sessions for five consecutive weeks.

3. Recently, the Sales Representative for my accounts promised my client that the operations team could and would perform a manual process without receiving approval from the Operations Manager.

   Recently, without receiving approval from the operations manager, the sales representative for my accounts promised my client the operations team could and would perform a manual process.

4. To begin operations immediately, the materials must be in the warehouse by Monday.

   So we can begin operations immediately, the materials must be in the warehouse by Monday.

Parallelism Practice (p. 164)

1. The current changes are proposed to facilitate the departmental filing system and *to create* more detailed address information.

2. This decision was based on low cost, instant availability, and *quality service*.

3. My accomplishments last quarter:

   a. Created more efficient accounting form;

   b. Conducted and *finalized* two important negotiations;

   c. *Fulfilled* your duties when you were on other assignments;

   d. *Developed* an urgent correspondence letter-routing system.

Sentence Errors Practice (p. 164)

Run-on sentences, fragments, comma splices/fused sentences, dangling modifiers, and parallel structure.

1. I will retain copies of your requests and should these people desire to schedule a class in January, I will place them at the top of the list. [*run-on*]

I will retain copies of your requests. Should these people desire to schedule a class in January, I will place them at the top of the list.

2. Our concerns are many, but heading the list is possible equipment damage and if something does happen to our #3 pump it is conceivable that we simply would not be able to bring on another pump, unless we could convince the electric company to crank up the voltage. [*run-on*]

   Our concerns are many, but heading the list is possible equipment damage. If something does happen to our #3 pump, it is conceivable that we simply would not be able to bring on another pump unless we could convince the electric company to crank up the voltage.

3. Hoping this will handle the problem. [*fragment*]

   I hope this option will handle the problem.

4. This is a rush, the report is due soon. [*comma splice*]

   This is a rush because the report is due soon.

5. In an effort to track the number of training hours the staff receives, I would appreciate a quarterly report from you listing employee name, course and/or seminar completed. Also the number of training hours for your direct reports. [*fragment*]

   To track the number of training hours the staff receives, I would appreciate a quarterly report from you listing employee name, course and/or seminar completed, and the number of training hours for your direct reports.

6. I'm sorry it wasn't with the rest of the papers, I checked with our Auditor's office and they were not holding it for any reason. [*comma splice*]

   I'm sorry it wasn't with the rest of the papers. I checked with our auditor's office, and the auditors were not holding it for any reason.

7. Not everyone has a firsthand personal knowledge of the dedicated staff you have, we see them everyday, and do appreciate your services. [*comma splice*]

   Not everyone has a firsthand, personal knowledge of the

dedicated staff you have. We see them every day and do appreciate your services.

8. By properly parking along one side of the alley adequate space would be available for one way traffic through the alley. [*dangling modifier*]

   Properly parking along one side of the alley would allow adequate space for one-way traffic through the alley.

9. If approved, Mrs. Smith requests two copies be returned to her office. [*dangling modifier*]

   If you approve, Mrs. Smith requests two copies be returned to her office.

10. I really like your staff; they have a great attitude, very friendly, and willing to help. [*parallelism*]

    I really like your staff; they have a great attitude, seem very friendly, and are willing to help.

11. However, the three principals decided that retention of heifers would allow for better quality of milk, command higher milk prices due to that quality, and with lower costs. [*parallelism*]

    However, the three principals decided that retention of heifers would create better quality milk, command higher prices due to that quality, and reduce production costs.

Practice in Correcting Sentences (p. 166)

Original

The bank where the fiber was damaged was allegedly located; and marked with orange paint by the technician. There was no apparent marking of a flag. Railway called for an identification on March 15, 200_, copies of one-call record placed by ATR are available. Another technician and the line supervisor could not verify that the area was marked by paint, and Railroad claimed there was no marking, so there is a major problem of non verification about the accuracy of the initial report. According to the technician, that allegedly marked the area, there was rain in the area three days prior to the Railroad drilling and the rain apparently washed the paint marks off of the area, leaving no sign and without proof.

Revised

The bank where the fiber was damaged was allegedly located and marked with orange paint by the technician. There was no apparent marking *with* a flag. Railway called for an identification on March 15, 200_. Copies of *the* one-call record placed by ATR are available. Another technician and the line supervisor could not verify that the area was marked by paint, and Railroad claimed there was no marking. *Therefore*, there is a major problem of nonverification about the accuracy of the initial report. According to the technician *who* allegedly marked the area, there was rain in the area three days prior to the Railroad drilling. *The* rain apparently washed the paint marks off of the area, leaving *no proof*.

Subject-Verb Agreement Practice (p. 173)

1. On July 2, 200_, a notification letter requesting receipts for this month were sent to you.

   *On July 2, 200_, a notification **letter** requesting receipts for this month **was** sent to you.*

2. As sonar technology and laser technology is implemented, additional OT or IT positions will have to be reclassified.

   *As **sonar technology** and **laser technology** are implemented, additional OT or IT positions will have to be reclassified.*

3. Completing the forms do not obligate you to become a volunteer.

   ***Completing the forms does** not obligate you to become a volunteer.*

4. However, assuming any motions are allowable, each are defeated.

   *However, assuming any motions are allowable, **each is** defeated.*

5. Neither Johnson, nor Peterson, were principals, officers, directors, shareholders, or managers of the company.

   *Neither **Johnson** nor **Peterson was a** principal, officer, director, shareholder, or manager of the company.*

6. If there is any further questions that I can answer for you please contact me at ext. 1234.

*If there **are** any further **questions** that I can answer for you, please contact me at ext. 1234.*

7. The alarm status of the switches are updated as status changes.

   *The alarm **status** of the switches **is** updated as status changes.*

Pronoun Practice (p. 178)

1. Within a few minutes she responded to my e-mail and submitted Pam a list. She is supposed to be working on that list today.

   *Within a few minutes she responded to my e-mail and sent Pam a list. **Pam** is supposed to be working on that list today.*

2. Susan and her agreed to accept responsibility for the United Way drive.

   *Susan and **she** agreed to accept responsibility for the United Way drive.*

3. Jim and I both agree that Lee, Jim, and myself should outline another approach to developing this business.

   *Jim and I both agree that Lee, Jim, and **I** should outline another approach to developing this business.*

4. Each band will perform their own style of music.

   *Each band will perform **its** own style of music.*

5. Our facilities are unique in that most are built in neighborhoods. This enables individuals, especially senior citizens and youth who are not mobile, easy access to quality social, fitness, and sports opportunities.

   *Our facilities are unique in that most are built in neighborhoods. **This proximity** enables individuals, especially senior citizens and youth who are not mobile, easy access to quality social, fitness, and sports opportunities.*

6. It would be appreciated if the contract could be prepared as soon as possible for consideration. This would be very helpful in that, it will be more cost effective to integrate the proposed project with other remodeling projects currently in progress.

*We would appreciate it if the contract could be prepared as soon as possible for consideration. **This timeliness would help integrate the proposed project with other remodeling projects in progress, thus being a more cost-effective approach.***

Word Formation Practice (p. 180)

Correct the following sentences, paying particular attention to errors in word formation—spelling, verb forms, subject-verb agreement, and pronoun usage:

1. But as the years have gone by, inflation and other factors has raised the cost of living.

   *But as the years have gone by, **inflation and other factors have** raised the cost of living.* [subject-verb agreement]

2. Mr. Johnson explained he had been involved in a vehicle accident and the other driver had left the scene of the accident. Mr. Johnson goes on to explain he followed the other driver to a location and was now located in front of a house but is not sure where he was.

   *Mr. Johnson **explained** he had been involved in a vehicle accident and the other driver had left the scene of the accident. Mr. Johnson **went** on to explain he followed the other driver to a location and was then in front of a house. **He was** not sure where he was.* [consistent verb tense]

3. John told you, Carman Simpson and myself, he had been at our location at the original meeting.

   *John told you, Carman Simpson, and **me that** he had been at our location **for** the original meeting.* [pronoun form, preposition choice]

4. Circles on the tabulation indicates low bids.

   ***Circles** on the tabulation **indicate** low bids.* [subject-verb agreement]

5. Each suspect stated they received payment for passing the counterfeited checks.

   ***Both suspects** stated they received payment for passing the counterfeited checks.* [noun-pronoun agreement]

6. Either I or Ron will let you know the results of the review and what our recommendation is.

   *Either Ron or I will let you know the results of the review and **our recommendation**.* [*noun-pronoun order and parallel structure*]

7. Financial support, like volunteer workers and effective speakers, are hard to get.

   ***Financial support**, like volunteer workers and effective speakers, **is** hard to get.* [*subject-verb agreement*]

8. Then each month your customer pays their bill, you will receive a monthly residual of up to $3 for the lifetime of the customers' subscription.

   *Then each month your **customers pay** their bills, you will receive a monthly residual of up to $3 for the lifetime of the customers' subscription.* [*noun-pronoun agreement*]

9. If a company fails to properly market their high-tech products they will often fail to meet their potential in the marketplace.

   *If a **company** fails to properly market **its** high-tech products, it will often fail to meet its potential in the marketplace.* [*noun-pronoun agreement*]

10. If there are less than five companies who post the type of crude then they are averaged.

    *If there are **fewer** than five companies **that** post **that** type of crude, then **the prices** are averaged.* [*word choice, pronoun choice, vague pronoun reference*]

11. Each of these subpoenas address separate categories of requested documents.

    ***Each** of these subpoenas **addresses** separate categories of requested documents.* [*subject-verb agreement*]

12. It would be appreciated if the contract could be prepared as soon as possible for consideration. This would be very helpful in that, it will be more cost effective to integrate the proposed project with other remodeling projects currently in progress.

    ***We would appreciate it** if the contract could be prepared as soon as possible for consideration. This **timeliness** would *be very helpful **since integrating** the proposed project with other remodeling projects currently in progress **will be more cost effective.** [broad pronoun reference]*

Practice Proofreading for Word Errors (p. 182)

Original

To: Jim Smith

From: Larry Johnson

Date: Jan. 3, 200_

Subject: New Vacation Schedule

Because every one in the Department try to take vacations at Christmas time, we are left understaffed at a busy time of the year. This effects the efficiency of the department and and makes it impossible to close the books before the end of the year report.

Next year there are a requirement that every employee should request vacation by their seniorty with only 5 allowed to vacation at Christmas. By seperating vacation times we can avoid the understaffing problem and still allows alot of flexibility in scheduling.

Revised

To: *Jim Smith*

From: *Larry Johnson*

Date: *Jan. 3, 200_*

Subject: *New Vacation Schedule*

Because everyone in the department tries to take a vacation at Christmas, we are left understaffed at a busy time of the year. This understaffing affects the efficiency of the department and makes it impossible to close the books before the end-of-the-year report.

Next year there is a requirement that every employee should request vacation by seniority, with only five people allowed a vacation at Christmas. By separating vacation times, we can avoid the understaffing problem and still allow a lot of flexibility in scheduling.

Proofreading Practice (p. 183)

Original

Every motor carrier according to the regulators have to establish a Employee Assistance Program (EAP) for their drivers and supervisor to use.

The EAP is suppose to consist of training programs for the supervisory personal and all drivers. It should include the affects and consequences of using illegal drugs and alcohol in regards to personal health, safety, and the work environment. The program also covers changes that indicates abuse and documentation of training given to the supervisory personal and drivers'.

If you now of an employee which needs help, have them call the following hot line number: 800-765-5151.

Revised

According to regulators, every motor carrier has to establish an Employee Assistance Program (EAP) for its drivers and supervisors to use.

The EAP is supposed to consist of training programs for supervisory personnel and all drivers. Training should include the consequences of using illegal drugs and alcohol in regard to personal health, safety, and work environment. The programs should also cover changes that indicate abuse and any documentation of training given to supervisory personnel and drivers.

If you know of employees who need help, have them call the following hotline number: 800-765-5151.

Punctuation and Mechanics Practice (p. 194)

[,]

1. We plan to use two people entering the same information on a diskette, then a software program will match the entries and produce a list of the ones that don't match.

   We plan to use two people entering the same information on a diskette.Then a software program will match the entries and produce a list of the ones that don't match.

2. If there is any way I can help please let me know.

If there is any way I can help, please let me know.

3. Although, not much I trust it will help out.

   Although not much, I trust it will help out.

4. Mary Jane in our International Department, has informed us that the Letter of Credit numbers are pre-issued.

   Mary Jane in our International Department has informed us that the letter of credit numbers are preissued.

5. Keys can be created in the user's own file allowing more efficient data processing.

   Keys can be created in the user's own file, allowing more efficient data processing.

6. Mr. Brown believes the return was filed in a timely manner; however, the taxpayer has no proof of this.

   Mr. Brown believes the return was filed in a timely manner; however, the taxpayer has no proof of this assertion.

7. We would like your response to the 6 findings and recommendations noted in our report, and in particular, to the items listed below.

   We would like your response to the six findings and recommendations noted in our report and, in particular, to the items listed below.

8. Their tanks are on control now and when the tank reaches a certain level a valve opens allowing fuel to flow to the tank.

   Their tanks are on control now, and when the tank reaches a certain level, a valve opens, allowing fuel to flow to the tank.

9. In closing the Architect, Mr. Smith asked that in lieu of an immediate decision or directive as we had originally intended, that some additional time be given for cost analysis and consideration.

   In closing, the architect, Mr. Smith, asked that in lieu of an immediate decision or directive as we had originally intended, some additional time be given for cost analysis and consideration.

[:]

10. This column will cover the three essential elements of unseating an industry leader, spot the opportunity, attack, and cover your backside.

    This column will cover the three essential elements of unseating an industry leader: spot the opportunity, attack, and cover your backside.

11. They are listed below in order of the farthest East down to the road;

    They are listed below in order of the farthest east down to the road:

12. These include: air quality, wildlife, land preservation and hazardous waste and many more factors affecting our ecological systems.

    These include air quality, wildlife, land preservation and hazardous waste, and many more factors affecting our ecological systems.

[;]

13. The job posting program in itself will entail producing and storing many items on a P.C.; including: the job posting form, log of applicants—placements and results, letters to candidates, and daily updates of statistics.

    The job posting program in itself will entail producing and storing many items on a PC, including the job posting form, log of applicants, placements and results, letters to candidates, and daily updates of statistics.

14. Submit a section showing the design through the building; including connection to the existing building.

    Submit a section showing the design through the building, including connection to the existing building.

[']

15. This amount was to cover taxpayers estimate of any additional tax still owed. At some point between April 1, 200_ and August 10, 200_, taxpayer's believe their return was filed.

This amount was to cover the taxpayers' estimate of any additional tax still owed. At some point between April 1 200_ and August 10, 200_, taxpayers believe their return was filed.

16. The assessors' office uses the addition and deletions sheet to reclassify property.

   The assessor's office uses the additions and deletions sheet to reclassify property.

17. Jones who has seven years experience in the small retail business expects the rental trend to dramatically shift to video games.

   Jones, who has seven years' experience in the small retail business, expects the rental trend to dramatically shift to video games.

18. An account executive for Famous Jewelry made a point to memorize his customer's wives' names and special events in their lives such as birthdays and anniversaries.

   An account executive for Famous Jewelry made a point to memorize his customers' wives' names and special events in their lives such as birthdays and anniversaries.

19. Please, look at this wording and let me know if its ok.

   Please look at this wording and let me know if it's okay.

20. ACME assures you of its' utmost commitment to provide you with quality and responsiveness in the products we deliver.

   ACME assures you of its utmost commitment to provide you with quality and responsiveness in the products we deliver.

[-]

21. The company has gone to great pains to minimize marketing related expenses and to shift the burden of producing marketing materials to our affiliates.

   The company has gone to great pains to minimize marketing-related expenses and to shift the burden of producing marketing materials to our affiliates.

22. You make several broad based, wide ranging, all encompassing statements without providing details for rational conclusions.

    You make several broad-based, wide-ranging, all-encompassing statements without providing details for rational conclusions.

23. I will contact you to set a follow up meeting.

    I will contact you to set a follow-up meeting.

24. The short and long term cost is significant.

    The short- and long-term cost is significant.

25. We would run our pre-approved radio ads "Boxing" and "Travel" using the 40 second version with a 20 second custom tag during the campaign.

    We would run our preapproved radio ads "Boxing" and "Travel," using the 40-second version with a 20-second custom tag during the campaign.

[abbr.]

26. The seminar will begin at 8:00 am, and end at 4:00 pm.

    The seminar will begin at 8:00 a.m. and end at 4:00 p.m.

27. We would like to meet monthly; eg. the first Tuesday.

    We would like to meet monthly, e.g., the first Tuesday.

[#/date]

28. The project took a total of 5 hours utilizing 10 CSR's at 30 minutes each.

    The project took a total of five hours utilizing ten CSRs at 30 minutes each.

29. There is a three (3) inch open ended pipe in place used to drain the levee.

    There is a three-inch, open-ended pipe in place used to drain the levee.

30. The date of February 21st has been confirmed for the off-site Senior Management meeting from 8:00 am to 12:00 noon.

February 21 has been confirmed for the off-site senior management meeting from 8:00 a.m. to 12:00 noon.

31. The 5 PC's that were separated from the main ring are running three different operating systems.

   The five PCs that were separated from the main ring are running three different operating systems.

32. We plan to extend the lease for a term of Ten (10) years at $20.00 per month on May 21st, 200_.

   We plan to extend the lease for a term of ten years at $20.00 per month on May 21, 200_.

[cap]

33. periodic check of hard copies will be made to verify inspections. (30 day max.)

   Periodic check of hard copies will be made to verify inspections (30-day maximum).

34. I plan to follow up on this Firm particularly in regard to APPR.

   I plan to follow up on this firm, particularly in regard to APPR.

35. John will be reviewing our proposal with the President of his company during the first week of March, 200_.

   John will be reviewing our proposal with the president of his company during the first week of March 200_.

36. We intend to determine the effect of the marketing effort on:

   + telephone responses
   + sales increase
   + short term profit

   We intend to determine the effect of the marketing effort on:

   + *Telephone responses*
   + *Sales increase*
   + *Short-term profit*

37. She is currently being trained on Tort Claims, Garnishments, Checking out Documents, Retrieving items from the vault and scanning documents.

    She is currently being trained on filing tort claims, requesting garnishments, checking out documents, retrieving items from the vault, and scanning documents.

38. You spoke with our Fraud Investigator Craig & Craig indicated to me that you thought that you had already paid for these charges.

    You spoke with our fraud investigator Craig, who indicated to me that you had already paid for these charges.

39. if you could check this for me i would appreciate it.
    thanks

    *If you could check this for me, I would appreciate it.
    Thanks.*

40. We know you will enjoy seeing our lovely City.

    We know you will enjoy seeing our lovely city.

Corrected Punctuation Practice: Figure 6-2 (p.197)

To: All Employees
From: Lee Winn
Subject: Corporate Policy
*Date: July 6, 200_*

It is official company policy that each branch must complete proper reports. This policy is further outlined in Company Procedure 2250. In addition, Ms Jones, our president, said in her memo of May 10, 2003, "Branch reports are the most important indicator of our company's success." According to our records, you have not forwarded reports on time, have filled out reports incorrectly, and have ignored our previous requests for prompt reports. To insure that your July report is in my office by the August 10 deadline, mark your calendar today. The Jones Company needs your cooperation in sending prompt, correct monthly reports. May we count on your cooperation?

Thanks,
Lee

Corrected Proofreading Practice: Figure 6-3 (p. 198)

August 18, 200_

Samantha Johnson
The Leading Company
P.O. Box 3456
Central City, *AR* 55512

Dear Ms Johnson*:*

In regard to the recent Request for Verification of Employment that you completed on Tim Swanson, we need additional information. *Box 11 (Probability of Continued Employment) must be filled in.*

If you desire, you can use a phrase like "we *cannot* comment" or "we are an at-will company." You should fill in the form we sent; otherwise, we *cannot* process your request.

Thank you for your prompt response to this *request.* If you have *further* questions, please don't hesitate to call.

Thank *you,*

Amy Sanders
Loan *Processor*

Revised Refining Practice: Figure 6-4 (p. 200)

ALL AMERICAN TELEPHONE COMPANY
Sun City, Florida

Mr. A. B. Reader
1104 Apple Avenue
Quality City, Florida 11111-2222

Dear Mr. Reader:

As we discussed on December 13, I am sending you a copy of the changes recommended for your long-distance communication needs. Your current AATC services are antiquated for your changing calling patterns, without the flexibility you need. AATC has committed to keep its customers in the forefront of ever-changing technology with the most economical services that we have to offer.

By taking advantage of the new enhancements, your company will benefit in five discount areas:

1. NPA = highest called area code = 10 percent discount to the highest called area code each month.
2. FNO = highest called country = 10 percent discount to the highest called country each month.
3. Intracompany = all calls made between company locations or all calling card calls back to main company location = 20 percent discount on all of these calls.
4. Volume Discounts = tapered between 5 percent and 15 percent = depending on total volume used each month.
5. Flex Option Discount = extra discount based on time and monthly commitments to AATC tapered between an extra 3 percent and 8.5 percent.

You will also enjoy the convenience of receiving only one bill because this service allows your company to tie all of its locations into one monthly bill. Thus, you can take advantage of a service previously available only to very large companies such as Sears or Avis.

The enclosed short comparison shows how your company is being billed now and what your costs are, compared to the new service billing enhancements. To have the new enhancements implemented, please contact me at 1 800-906-1111, ext. 7654, or 504-323-0000.

Sincerely,

James Jones

Fundamentals

Most people are better writers than they think. They have a basic understanding of the language, with the logical skills good writing requires. Problems arise not from incompetence but from haste—usually in the prewriting and rewriting stages. *The Writing Coach* assumes you have certain fundamentals—the knowledge you need to get started and then begin practicing. This chapter backstops those fundamentals with two additional resources:

- A list of useful references with more specialized books, articles, and on-line sites that treat subjects in more depth.

- A very general summary of the structure and terminology of English grammar.

Call on these resources when you need them.

CHAPTER 8—FUNDAMENTALS

USEFUL REFERENCES

Style and Correctness Guides

American Heritage College Dictionary. Boston: Houghton Mifflin, 2000. Any recent dictionary will give current guidance on spelling and definitions. Replacing your dictionary every ten years will keep you up to date on current practice.

The Chicago Manual of Style. University of Chicago Press, 1993. Guide to punctuation and mechanics for academic presses.

Goldstein, Norm, ed. *The Associated Press Stylebook and Briefing on Media Law.* Cambridge, MA: Perseus Publishing, 2000. The stylebook for journalists on punctuation, mechanics, and spelling.

Gunning, Robert, and Douglas Mueller. *How to Take the Fog out of Business Writing.* Chicago: Dartnell Corporation, 1994. A classic booklet on writing clear sentences.

Hacker, Diana. *A Writer's Reference.* Boston: Bedford/St. Martin's, 1999. A very reader-friendly college text.

Kolln, Martha, and Robert Funk. *Understanding English Grammar.* New York: Longman, 2002. An excellent textbook on the structure of English words and sentences.

Sabin, William A. *The Gregg Reference Manual.* New York: Glencoe McGraw-Hill, 2001. The best business reference for basic grammar, punctuation, and mechanics.

Strunk, William. *The Elements of Style.* Revised by E. B. White. Boston: Allyn & Bacon, 2000. The Classic. On-line at <http://www.columbia.edu>.

Williams, Joseph M. *Style: Ten Lessons in Clarity and Grace.* New York: Longman, 2002. A very useful guide to editing.

Writing in Special Contexts

Flower, Linda. *Problem Solving Strategies for Writing in College and the Community.* Boston: Heinle & Heinle, 1997.

Garner, Bryan A. *Legal Writing in Plain English: A Text with Exercises.* University of Chicago Press, 2001.

Gopen, George D., and Judith A. Swan. "The Science of Scientific Writing," *American Scientist, 78* (1990): 550–558.

Harty, Kevin J. *Strategies for Business and Technical Writing.* Boston: Allyn & Bacon, 1999. Collection of articles about workplace writing, including "The File Cabinet Has a Sex Life: Insights of a Professional Writing Consultant" by Lee Clark Johns.

Kilian, Crawford. *Writing for the Web: Writers' Edition.* Self-Counsel Writing Series, 1999.

Kramer, Melinda. *Business Communication in Context: Principles and Practice.* New Jersey: Prentice Hall, 2001.

Mathes, J. C., and Dwight W. Stevenson. *Designing Technical Reports: Writing for Audiences in Organizations.* Boston: Allyn & Bacon, 1991. The classic in technical writing.

Matthies, Leslie H. *The New Playscript Procedure: Management Tool for Action.* Stamford, CT: Office Publications, Inc., 1977. A breakthrough book that is out of print. For brief summary, see <http://www.jeanweber.com>.

Munter, Mary. *Guide to Managerial Communicatons: Effective Business Writing and Speaking.* New Jersey: Prentice Hall, 2002.

Zimmerman, Donald E., and David G. Clark. *The Random House Guide to Technical and Scientific Communication.* New York: Random House, 1987.

On-line References

<http://www.bartleby.com>. Free portal to great books and references on-line; named Best Literary Resource for 2002.

Merriam-Webster Online. Springfield, MA. <http://www.m-w.com>. Excellent Language Center that delivers quick dictionary and thesaurus reference services. Also offers free "Word of the Day" e-mail for vocabulary-building.

Kilian, Crawford. "Content Spotlight," <http://www.content-exchange.com>. Current articles on Web writing.

Fundamentals

Nielsen, Jakob. <http://www.useit.com>. Current research on Internet communication issues.

Purdue Online Writing Lab (OWL). <http://owl.english. purdue.edu>. Extensive advice and practice on grammar issues.

Roget's Thesaurus of English Words and Phrases. Nothing Limited, 1996. <http://thesaurus.reference.com/>.

Sun Microsystems, *Writing for the Web.* <http://www.sun.com>.

General Interest

Forbes, Malcolm, "How to Write a Business Letter." In Kevin J. Harty (ed.), *Strategies for Business and Technical Writing* (pp. 108–111). Boston: Allyn & Bacon, 1999.

Hayakawa, S. I. *Language in Thought and Action.* New York: Harcourt Brace Jovanovich, 1978. *The* book on understanding the nature of language and its impact on society.

Wallace, David Foster. "Tense Present: Democracy, English and the Wars over Usage." *Harper's* (April 2001): 39–58. Highly readable analysis of the usage "war" between grammatical hardliners and permissives.

Graphics and Document Design

Parker, Roger C. *The Makeover Book: 101 Design Solutions for Desktop Publishing.* Chapel Hill: Ventana Press, 1989. Out of print, but useful for redesigning forms if you can find it.

Tufte, Edward R. *The Visual Display of Quantitative Information.* Cheshire, CT: Graphics Press, 1983. Like later Tufte books, an outstanding guide to translating words for the visual age.

Williams, Robin. *The Non-Designer's Design Book: Design and Typographic Principles for the Visual Novice.* Berkeley: Peachpit Press, 1994. Very helpful for "word people" who use graphic elements.

GRAMMAR FUNDAMENTALS

Understanding Sentences

Most people think that they don't know grammar. In fact, they groan when asked, "How many of you think you are experts in English grammar?" But they *are* experts—just as you are. Every time you, as a native speaker of the language, say or write something, you demonstrate a sophisticated knowledge of the "formulas" of word and sentence formation. You acquired these formulas as a young child learning to speak. In a sense, they are the program that runs your language computer. So, you know English grammar; you just don't know that you know it.

Most of the time, if you listen to what you have written, you will find any errors that are there. If it does not sound right, it probably is not. This section outlines the key formulas in your English language program. For more in-depth information or complex questions, consult a good grammar text, such as *Understanding English Grammar* by Martha Kolln and Robert Funk.

Sentence Cores

The core of a sentence is its structural heart, the basic components of a subject and verb, plus possibly an object or complement. The simplest sentence contains only these core elements. However, more complex ideas require adding modifiers to build the details of your sentence. To be most effective, the sentence should focus the main idea in the sentence core. The modifiers are added as adjectives and adverbs, phrases and clauses.

English has three basic types of sentence cores. Their differences lie in what follows the verb: nothing or only modifiers; a direct object; or a complement. The verb type depends on what follows it (see Table 8-1).

Key Sentence Terms

The **subject** is the "actor" in the sentence. It is usually a noun, but can be a verbal phrase or a noun dependent clause.

The **verb**, or **predicate**, states the act or state of being. It is the power drive of the sentence.

The **direct object** receives the action of the verb.

Table 8-1. Sentence Cores

Sentence Core				Verb Type
Core 1	**Subject — Verb** People work. Times change. She is early. X Stop!			**Intransitive** verb — does not carry action to a direct object.
Core 2	**Subject — Verb — Object** Tom hit the ball. He knew the answer.			**Transitive** verb — carries action to a direct object.
	Subject — Verb — Indirect Object — Direct Object She sent me the report. He asked me a question.			
	Subject — Verb — Direct Object — Object Complement Mary made the vendor happy. He called the report a triumph.			
Core 3	**Subject — Verb — Complement** Millicent is chairman. Reports are long. He looks tired.			**Linking** verb — links the subject to the complement, which names [*predicate nominative*] or describes [*predicate adjective*] the subject.

The **indirect object** receives the direct object. It can be replaced by a "to" or "for" prepositional phrase:

> *She sent me a card* ➤ *She sent a card to me.*
>   IO   DO   DO   OP

The **object complement** follows and either renames (noun) or describes (adjective) the direct object:

> *The committee named me chairperson. Then they proclaimed the*
> *site vacant.*   DO   OC
> DO   OC

The **complement** follows a linking verb (forms of *to be, seem, appear*) and either renames the subject (**predicate nominative**) or describes the subject (**predicate adjective**).

A clause is a group of words that includes a subject and a predicate. In other words, it is a sentence core.

■ An **independent** clause (or **sentence**) can stand alone because it expresses a complete thought. Example: *The manager gathered the data.*

■ A **dependent** clause cannot stand alone because it has an introductory word that requires it to be connected to a sentence. The introductory words include:

—**subordinating conjunctions** (*because, if, when, although, since, . . .*), which make the clause act like an adverb — *When the manager gathered the data, . . .* , or

—**relative pronouns** (*who, which, that, whom, whose*), which make the clause act like an adjective or noun — *The manager who gathered the data . . .*

A dependent clause that is not connected to an independent clause is called a **fragment**.

Phrases are groups of words that do not have a subject and a verb. They modify (or describe) other words in the sentence.

Prepositional phrases begin with a preposition and end with a noun (**the object of the preposition**). These phrases act like adjectives and adverbs, describing either nouns, verbs, or adjectives. Example: *Before the competition, the engineers from the head office ran the test on the slick, but fast track.*

Verbal phrases begin with a verb form, but do the jobs of other parts of speech within a sentence.

■ **Infinitive phrases**, formed with *to + the base form* of the verb, act like nouns, adjectives, and adverbs. Example: *To go slowly was against his nature.*

■ **Participial phrases**, using the *–ing* or *–en* form of the verb, act like adjectives to describe nouns. Example: *The opening roar meant the crowd had gathered, driven to the track in their gas-guzzling cars.*

■ **Gerund phrases**, using the *–ing* form of the verb, take noun roles in the sentence, such as subject, direct object, object of the preposition, and so on. Example: *Before starting their engines, the test drivers checked their cars thoroughly.*

Sentence types depend on the number and types of clauses. Using different sentence lengths and types to vary your sentence structure creates a more interesting style.

■ **Simple sentences** have only one independent clause, although they may have many modifiers. "Simple" does not mean "short." Example: *The engineer riding in the lead car was overwhelmed by the excitement.*

■ **Compound sentences** have two or more independent clauses. Example: *The spectators saw the lead car beginnning to weave; however, they did not expect to see it crash.*

■ **Complex sentences** have one independent clause and one or more dependent clauses. Example: *Although safety was a prime concern, no one had checked the tires.*

■ **Compound-complex sentences** have two or more independent clauses and one or more dependent clauses. Example: *Because the accident was severe, the federal highway regulators wanted immediate answers on how they could prevent future accidents, but the engineers had not yet finished their causal analysis.*

Understanding Word Formation

Structure also plays a role in creating the meaning of words. Some words—the bricks of the language—change their **form** and thus change meaning. Other words—the mortar of the sentence—hold the form words together and create the **structure** of the sentence. Pronouns do both: they change form, depending on their use in the sentence, and they create the structural link for adjective dependent clauses.

Parts of Speech. Table 8-2 summarizes the suffixes we use to create the regular form words in English and the structure words that go with each type of form word to create phrases and clauses. These word formation rules will help you identify errors in spelling, word choice, verb formation, subject-verb agreement, and pronoun usage. Refer to Chapter 6 for details about usage errors.

Table 8-2. Parts of Speech

Form Words	Structure Words
Nouns — the name of a person, place, or thing **-s** plural — *girls* **-'s** singular possessive — *girl's book* **-s'** plural possessive — *girls' books*	**Noun Determiners** — indicate *"here comes a noun"* (*a, an, the, all, both, first, one, possessives…*) **Prepositions** — create prepositional phrases, with nouns as their objects (*in, out, for, to, of, around, before, except, down, into, on…*)
Verbs — show action or state of being **-s** 3rd person singular, present tense *He likes; he sees; she is* **-ed** past tense and past participle of regular verbs *He liked; he had liked* **-en** past participle of many irregular verbs *He had seen; he had written* **-ing** present participle *He is liking; he is seeing*	**Auxiliaries** — create verb phrases that indicate: • future tense (*will, shall*) • perfect (*have*) • progressive (*be*) • passive voice (*be*) • conditional (*can, could, may, might*) • obligation (*should, ought to, must*) • other specialized meanings (*do, would*)
Adjectives — describe a noun **-er** comparative (two items) *She made the wiser choice of the two.* **-est** superlative (more than two) *She made the wisest choice of all.*	**Qualifiers** — limit the adjective (*very, quite, rather . . .*) *It was a very quiet day.* *She was quite wise.*
Adverbs — describe a verb or adjective **-er** comparative (two) *He ran slower than I.* **-est** superlative (more than two) *She ran slowest of all.*	**Qualifiers** — limit the adverb (*very, quite, rather…*) *I ran rather slowly.*
	Conjunctions — connect words, phrases, and clauses • Coordinating — *and, or, but, yet, so, for* • Subordinating — *when, if, because, since, although, whereas . . .* • Correlative — come in pairs — *either/or, neither/nor, not only/but also*
	Interrogatives — introduce questions (*Who, What, When, Where, Why, How . . .*)
	Expletives —placeholder words in a sentence (*There, that, as . . .*) *There was one suggestion.* *We hope that you come.*
Pronouns — take the place of a noun **Personal pronouns** — *I, you, he, she, it, we, you, they* **Relative pronouns** — *who, whom, which, that, whoever, whichever* **Reflexive and intensive pronouns** — *myself, yourself, himself, herself . . .* **Demonstrative pronouns** — *this, that, these, those* **Indefinite pronouns** — *each, all, everyone, everybody, some, both . . .*	

Forming Verbs

Verbs power the sentence. In English, they state the action (meaning), time (tense), condition (mode), and relation to the subject (voice). Simple verbs have only tense. More complex forms may have meaning plus all three:

- **Tenses** — present, past, or future

  Present — *She sings in the chorus.*

  Past — *She sang in the chorus.*

  Future — *She will sing in the chorus.*

- **Modes** — perfect (completed action) or progressive (on-going action)

  Past perfect — *She had sung beautifully before she fainted.*

  Past progressive — *She was singing beautifully when she fainted.*

- **Voices** — active or passive; applies only to verbs that take a direct object.

  Active — *She prepared her song for the concert.*

  Passive — *Her song was prepared for the concert.*

The five verb forms are used to create all verb phrases:

	Ending	*Form*	*Example*
1.	Ø = no ending	the base form, or infinitive	look see
2.	the -*s* form *base* + -*s*	3rd person singular, present tense	looks sees
3.	the -*ing* form *base* + -*ing*	present participle	looking seeing
4.	the -*ed* form	past tense	looked (*regular*) saw (*irregular*)
5.	the -*en* form	past participle	looked (*regular*) seen (*irregular*)

Refer to Chapter 6 for the list of the irregular verbs.

All verb phrases are created with these basic forms plus **auxiliaries** (helping verbs) in a certain order. This order is the same, whether you create a one-word simple present or past tense verb, or a complex series of auxiliaries and the main verb.

Verb Phrase Formula—A verb must have a tense and main verb to form the predicate of a sentence: **Tense + Main Verb**. Only two tenses, simple present and simple past, use just one word (see Table 8-3).

Table 8-3. Simple Present and Simple Past Tense

Subject	Present Tense	Past Tense
I	look	looked
I	see	saw
He	looks (*3rd singular*)	looked
He	sees (*3rd singular*)	saw

The formula in Table 8-4 demonstrates how we create more complex verb phrases. A series of auxiliaries plus the main verb adds special meanings, such as future tense, completed (*perfect mode*), or on-going (*progressive mode*) action. The first word in the series always shows the tense (T); the last word is always the main verb (MV). The arrows in Table 8-4 indicate that each auxiliary requires that the next verb have a certain form. Read from left to right to see how the auxiliaries shape the meaning. Then try reading one out of order. The verb will sound garbled—indicating that you know this formula.

Table 8-4. Complex Tense Formation

T *tense*	Modal ⟶ Ø auxiliary *future* or *conditional*	have ⟶ –en *perfect* *(completed action)*	be ⟶ –ing *progressive* *(on-going action)*	MV *main verb*
John... *subject*				
past				... **looked** at the magazine...
present				... **sees** an opportunity ...
future	... **will**			**see** you now.
present perfect		... **has**		**looked** for the answer.
past perfect		... **had**		**seen** him before.
future perfect	... **will**	**have**		**seen** him before I arrive.
present progressive			... **is**	**looking** fine.
past progressive			... **was**	**looking** everywhere.
past perfect progressive		... **had**	**been**	**seeing** her for months.
present perfect progressive		... **has**	**been**	**looking** tired lately.
future perfect progressive	... **will**	**have**	**been**	**looking** for her all night by the time we arrive.
present progressive conditional	... **may**		**be**	**looking** for a job.
past perfect progressive conditional	... **should**	**have**	**been**	**looking** when he crossed the street.

Passive Voice Formation—With verbs in the passive voice, the **subject** of the sentence **receives** the action, and the actor is in an actual or implied *"by"* prepositional phrase (see Table 8-5).

Table 8-5. Passive Voice Formation

| Subject | Passive Voice S-V | | Active Voice S-V-O |
	be → -en	Main Verb	
Susan	**is** (*present tense*)	**admired** by all.	All admire Susan.
The report	**was** (*past tense*)	**written** in Spanish.	He wrote the report in Spanish.
The test	**will be** (*future tense*)	**given** today.	I will give the test today.

Pronouns

Use personal pronouns in the correct case, or form. The case depends on the pronoun's function in the sentence, as shown in Table 6-3 in Chapter 6 (p. 176).

The **relative pronouns**—*who, whom, which,* and *that*—introduce dependent adjective clauses, relating the adjective clause to the noun it describes. To be used correctly, the pronoun must clearly refer to a noun preceding it. Chapter 6 contains the rules for correct pronoun usage.

Index